EPA500-R-96-002
December 1996

ENVIRONMENTAL JUSTICE, URBAN REVITALIZATION, AND BROWNFIELDS:

THE SEARCH FOR AUTHENTIC SIGNS OF HOPE

**A Report on the
"Public Dialogues on Urban Revitalization and Brownfields:
Envisioning Healthy and Sustainable Communities"**

*National Environmental Justice Advisory Council
Waste and Facility Siting Subcommittee
Charles Lee, Chair*

A Federal Advisory Committee to the U.S. Environmental Protection Agency

 **NATIONAL ENVIRONMENTAL JUSTICE ADVISORY COUNCIL**

Carol Browner, Administrator   July 29, 1996
U.S. Environmental Protection Agency
401 M Street, SW
Washington, DC 20460

Dear Administrator Browner:

Attached, please find a copy of the final report, *"Environmental Justice, Urban Revitalization, and Brownfields: The Search for Authentic Signs of Hope."* At the May 29-31 meeting of the National Environmental Justice Advisory Council in Detroit, Michigan, the Council discussed the Waste and Facility Siting Subcommittee's report, *"Environmental Justice, Urban Revitalization, and Brownfields: The Search for Authentic Signs of Hope."* The Council has agreed to endorse the report, as reflected in a formal mail vote, and to transmit it to you. The purpose of this letter is to request that you review the report and address the action items identified in the report.

We are transmitting this document to you on behalf of the members of the NEJAC. We do so with sincere gratitude for the many persons who gave tirelessly of their time, energy, and expertise to make the NEJAC Public Dialogues on Urban Revitalization and Brownfields an outstanding success.

The report follows up on, and analyzes the findings from, the public dialogues on urban revitalization and Brownfields which were held in June and July 1995. As you read this report, we hope you will appreciate the reasons for our sense of profound urgency regarding the issues raised in the report.

Sincerely,

Richard Moore, Chair
National Environmental Justice Advisory Council

Charles Lee, Chair
NEJAC Waste and Facility Siting Subcommittee

cc: NEJAC Council Members

DEDICATION

Dr. Jean Sindab, Director of Environmental and Economic Justice/Hunger Concerns for the National Council of Churches and a member of the National Environmental Justice Advisory Council, passed away on January 8, 1996 after a long and hard battle with cancer. Those of us who knew her well are deeply saddened by our loss. In reflecting upon Jean's life, we realized that this report attempts to speak to some of the issues at the very core of her life's work. For example, she and I worked on developing an Urban Strategies Initiative for the National Council of Churches in the wake of events in South Central Los Angeles. She organized the Black Church Network on Environmental and Economic Justice.

Jean chose to serve on the Waste and Facility Siting Subcommittee because of her interest in the job creation aspects of the Brownfields issue. Her passion was the plight of inner city youth, and she clearly understood the linkages between living in degraded physical environments, mass alienation, and destructive violence. It can be said that her life's work was dedicated to the constant search for authentic signs of hope. Many formative concepts behind this report germinated during our discussions years before the establishment of the National Environmental Justice Advisory Council. Jean struggled mightily to attend all the NEJAC "Public Dialogues on Urban Revitalization and Brownfields." She especially liked the idea of "Envisioning Healthy and Sustainable Communities." Despite her illness, she was able to attend our Public Dialogue in Boston, and we were indeed graced by her presence.

We believe that the vision which this report hopes to articulate is one she embraced and dedicated her life to help realize. She helped me to formulate the question which pervades this report: Can the restoration of the physical environment become an anchoring point for economic, social, cultural, and spiritual renewal? In very real sense, she contributed to this report in ways she may never know. Therefore, we dedicate this report to the "living" memory of the life and work of Dr. Jean Sindab.

Charles Lee

CONTENTS

The vision of environmental justice is the development of a holistic, bottomup, community-based, multi-issue, cross-cutting, integrative, and unifying paradigm for achieving healthy and sustainable communities--both urban and rural. In the context of ecological peril, economic dysfunctionality, infrastructure decay, racial polarization, social turmoil, cultural disorientation, and spiritual malaise which grips urban America at the end of the 20th century, environmental justice is indeed a much needed breath of fresh air. Tragically, many positive developments have been rendered invisible behind the curtain of a sensationalism-oriented mass media. However, there is no denying that great resilience exists in the economic, cultural, and spiritual life of America's communities. There are many stellar accomplishments, entrepreneurial successes, and significant victories--both big and small. Hence, an abiding goal of the Public Dialogues on Urban Revitalization and Brownfields was the **constant search for authentic signs of hope**.

Background

In 1995, the National Environmental Justice Advisory Council (NEJAC) Waste and Facility Siting Subcommittee and the U.S. Environmental Protection Agency co-sponsored a series of public hearings entitled, "Public Dialogues on Urban Revitalization and Brownfields: Envisioning Healthy and Sustainable Communities." The Public Dialogues were held in five cities: Boston, Massachusetts; Philadelphia, Pennsylvania; Detroit, Michigan; Oakland, California; and Atlanta, Georgia. They were intended to provide for the first time an opportunity for environmental justice advocates and residents of impacted communities to systematically provide input regarding issues related to the EPA's Brownfields Economic Redevelopment Initiative.

More than 500 persons from community groups, government agencies, faith groups, labor, philanthropies, universities, banks, businesses, and other institutions participated in a "systematic attempt to stimulate a new and vigorous public discourse about developing strategies, partnerships, models, and projects for ensuring healthy and sustainable communities in America's urban centers and demonstrating their importance to the nation's environmental and economic future." Representatives from 15 federal agencies as well as state and local, and tribal governments participated.

Concerns were raised by members of the public about the Brownfields Initiative, i.e., whether or not the Brownfields issue was a "smoke screen" for gutting cleanup standards, environmental regulations, and liability safeguards. Heretofore, public policy discourse around the Brownfields issue has revolved around removing barriers to real estate and investment transactions at sites where there exists toxic contamination concerns--real or perceived.

There is hope that the Brownfields Initiative will provide an opportunity to (1) stem the ecologically untenable, environmentally damaging, socially costly, and racially divisive phenomenon of urban sprawl and Greenfields development; (2) provide focus to a problem which by its very nature is inextricably linked to environmental justice, for example, the physical deterioration of the nation's urban areas; (3) allow communities to offer their vision of what redevelopment should look like; (4) apply environmental justice principles to the development of a new generation of environmental policy capable of meeting complex challenges such as Brownfields and the existence of a severe crisis in urban America; and (5) bring greater awareness and opportunities for building partnerships between EPA and communities and other stakeholders. As a result, EPA committed itself to supporting a sustained dialogue on Brownfields and environmental justice issues.

EPA already has begun to address concerns raised during the Public Dialogues. For example, EPA revised the criteria for applying for the Brownfields pilots based on comments provided by the NEJAC.

The comments emphasize community involvement and recommend that the extent of community involvement be verified. In February 1996, EPA hosted the Brownfields Pilots National Workshop to increase the coordination on issues related to Brownfields and environmental justice. EPA has begun a focused dialogue on developing mechanisms to ensure linkages between Federal Facilities restoration with urban revitalization/Brownfields. These efforts lay an important foundation for EPA and other agencies to address the recommendations in this report.

Environmental Justice and Brownfields

Abandoned commercial and industrial properties called "Brownfields," which dot the urban landscape, are overwhelmingly concentrated in people of color, low-income, indigenous peoples, and otherwise marginalized communities. By their very nature, Brownfields are inseparable from issues of social inequity, racial discrimination and urban decay--specifically manifested in adverse land use decisions, housing discrimination, residential segregation, community disinvestment, infrastructure decay, lack of educational and employment opportunity, and other issues.

The existence of degraded and hazardous physical environments in people of color, low-income, indigenous peoples, and otherwise disenfranchised communities is apparent and indisputable. The physical elements of such environments, in part or in whole, have contributed to human disease and illness, negative psycho-social impact, economic disincentive, infrastructure decay, and overall community disintegration. Brownfields are merely one aspect of this phenomenon.

Environmental justice and Brownfields are inextricably linked; the inescapable context for discussion of the Brownfields issue is environmental justice and urban revitalization. At the core of an environmental justice perspective is recognition of the interconnectedness of the physical environment to the overall economic, social, human, and cultural/spiritual health of a community. The vision of environmental justice is the development of a paradigm to achieve socially equitable, environmentally healthy, economically secure, psychologically vital, spiritually whole, and ecologically sustainable communities. To this end, Brownfields redevelopment must be linked to helping address this broader set of community needs and goals. It should be noted that revitalization, as we define it, does not lead to displacement of populations through gentrification that often results from redevelopment policies.

Key issues in the Brownfields debate are:

- • Understanding the Nature of Urban Environments

- • The Ecological Importance of Urban Areas

- • Reframing the Urban/Rural Dichotomy

- • Confronting the Issue of Race and Class

- • Urban Revitalization and Community-Driven Models of Redevelopment

- • Community Mapping and Community-Based Environmental Protection

- • Executive Order 12898 and Government Reinvention

- • Environmental Justice and the Next Generation of Environmental Protection.

The Brownfields issue compels an examination of development patterns on a regional basis, offering a vision of making links between different communities across the region with common perspectives on social issues as well as environmental issues, and developing strategies to address the polarization between suburban and inner city areas. In order to achieve equal protection under the law, we must develop integrative analytical models for examining how benefits and burdens have been distributed in American society. For example, past zoning and land use decisions are compounded by transportation policies which spur urban sprawl, disincentives for investment, and exacerbation of preexisting racial and social disparities.

Such an approach has important ramifications for the development of strategies, partnerships, models, and pilot projects. It requires a firm commitment towards the goals of environmental justice and must involve the community as an equal partner. In addition, it must integrate activities of all federal agencies as well as their state, local, and tribal counterparts. Through these Public Dialogues, communities have articulated a highly compelling vision of the future that speaks to the entire federal government, as well as state, local, tribal governments. These recommendations were developed within the framework of a number of overarching questions which emerged from testimony at the Public Dialogues on Urban Revitalization and Brownfields.

Recommendations

Although this report provides an extensive set of recommendations, it attempts as its "heart and soul" to illustrate the organic interrelationships between **people**, **community**, **social institutions**, **government**, and **public policy**. The "glue" which sustains these relationships is a system of values which treats the hopes and aspirations of people and families as important, exhibits compassion and care for the less fortunate, and supports the social fabric which enables communities to be healthy, wholesome, and sustainable.

When environmental justice posited the notion that "people must speak for themselves" about an environment defined as the place where "we live, where we work, and where we play," it established a framework for functionally bridging the key components of emerging environmental policy, i.e., ecosystem management and community-based environmental protection, equal protection, pollution prevention, cumulative risk and sound science, programmatic integration and government reinvention, and accountability to the public. This fact needs to be elevated as a major tenet of emerging environmental policy.

Moreover, the Brownfields issue compels an examination of integration between place-based approaches to environmental protection with sector-based approaches and their implications for industrial policy. More likely than not, any industrial sector which has entered its second generation and beyond will have large numbers of large numbers of Brownfield sites. Environmental and economic policy must take into account the benefits and costs of the entire "life-cycle" of an industrial sector or facility. Failure to do so results in passing on costs to future generations. For this reason, pollution prevention must be integrated as an overarching principle into all Brownfields projects.

Environmental justice is predicated upon the fact that the health of the members of a community, both individually and collectively, is a product of physical, social, cultural, and spiritual factors. It provides a key to understanding an integrative environmental policy which treats our common ecosystem as the basis for all life (human and non-human) and activity (economic and otherwise).

Recommendation highlights include:

I. Public Participation and Community Vision

1. Informed and Empowered Community Involvement:

Early, ongoing, and meaningful public participation is the hallmark of sound public policy and decision making. The community most directly impacted by a problem or a project is inherently qualified to participate in the decision-making process. Mechanisms must be established to ensure their full participation, including training and support for community groups, technical assistance grants, community advisory groups, and others.

• •   *Support sustained and structured public dialogue on Brownfields and environmental justice on all levels.*

• •   *Institute policies and performance measures which encourage program personnel and policy makers to spend substantive time in neighborhoods as a regular part of their work so that there is understanding of real problems, concerns, and aspirations of community residents.*

• •   *Undertake special outreach efforts to overlooked groups.*

2. Community Vision/Comprehensive Community Based Planning:

There exists within local communities highly coherent, vibrant, and compelling visions for achieving healthy and sustainable communities. Brownfields and all community revitalization efforts must be based upon such visions. The public dialogues articulated the importance of developing holistic, multi-faceted, interactive, and integrative community-based planning models.

•   *Acknowledge community-based planning as a critical methodology for environmental protection and promote its use both inside and outside the Agency.*

•   *Convene a national roundtable on strategies for application and development of geographic information systems and community mapping tools.*

•   *Develop guidance for incorporation of community-based planning and community visioning into Community-Based Environmental Protection initiatives.*

3. Role and Participation of Youth:

Young people provide great energy, creativity, and a sense of fresh vision. Urban revitalization/ Brownfields issues are matters of great concern to young people. Issues of healthy and sustainable communities are questions of a viable future. Government and social institutions have a moral obligation to ensure a world fit for all children--present and future.

•   *Form the requisite partnerships both inside and outside of government to better understand and address urban revitalization/Brownfields issues of concern to youth.*

•   *Through the Brownfields initiative, integrate environmental activities and career development with targeted environmental justice and urban revitalization strategies.*

•   *Designate •youth• as a formal stakeholder category for federal advisory committees and other multi-stakeholder public participation processes.*

II. Key Issue Areas

4. Equal Protection:

The urban revitalization/Brownfields issue focuses attention on yet another important set of equal protection issues, i.e., urban sprawl. Many federal programs have widened racial and socio-economic divisions in society by promoting disinvestment and placing substantial indirect burdens on communities and local economies.

In certain urban areas, urban sprawl is infringing upon nearby Tribal lands and, as such, is creating direct burdens on environmental, social, economic, and cultural values. In other urban areas, Tribal governments have won land claim settlements that provide for Tribal acquisition of urban lands that have included contaminated and potentially contaminated commercial and industrial areas. It is imperative that local jurisdictions that are located next to Tribal land pay attention to the concerns of the Tribal governments, as well as its Tribal community members. Urban revitalization and Brownfields programs must recognize ceded lands, fee lands, and all lands possessing historical, cultural, and spiritual values.

- • *Develop analytical models of the distributive impacts of federal programs which promote urban sprawl and incorporate such analyses into National Environmental Policy Act (NEPA) Environmental Justice Guidance.*

- • *Examine use of Title VI of the Civil Rights Act of 1964 with respect to federal support in areas of community reinvestment, fair housing, equal business opportunity, financing, and health protection.*

- • Identify all Tribal lands that are impacted by urban sprawl and evaluate barriers against equal protection.

5. Public Health, Environmental Standards, and Liability:

Public health and environmental protection are matters of primary concern to communities. In areas which suffer a long history of noxious land uses, illegal dumping, and lack of health and safety enforcement, priority must be given to ensuring that areas are safe for redevelopment as the first step in urban revitalization and brownfield redevelopment efforts. At this point, the public health has yet to be a real part of the urban revitalization/Brownfields discourse.

- • *Establish mechanisms which ensure a primary role for impacted communities in the decision-making process regarding public health and environmental protection issues.*

- • *Strengthen right-to-know, enforcement and compliance activity in impacted communities.*

- • *Support several Brownfields projects where the key component is assessment of health risks on a community-wide basis.*

- • *Conduct a series of dialogues on integration of public health and planning for purposes of achieving true urban revitalization with healthy and sustainable Brownfields redevelopment.*

6. Job Creation, Training, and Career Development:

Brownfields redevelopment must be coordinated with broader strategies of job creation, training; and career development which produce demonstrable benefits for the host community. Coordination and cooperation among government (federal, state, tribal, and local), business/industry, community-based organizations, labor unions, faith groups, and the community at large is mandatory in order to leverage resources and promote maximum benefit. Everyone benefits if they are unified and taking actions towards a common goal, i.e., a vibrant, safe, healthy, and sustainable community.

- • *Make use of the momentum generated by the Brownfields issue and provide leadership in building partnerships and coalitions which result in locally based job creation, entrepreneurial development, and sustainable careers.*

- • *Support efforts to ensure worker health and safety.*

7. Land Use:

Historical land use decisions based upon race have played a powerful role in shaping communities with large numbers of Brownfields. Inadequate zoning protection is a matter of paramount importance to impacted communities and environmental justice. It is critical that this social context be fully understood and addressed before embarking upon a national strategy of urban redevelopment. In so doing, common interests must be found across urban and suburban lines to develop a mutually compatible and supportive policy and program agendas.

- • *Examine land use patterns of an entire metropolitan area or region surrounding Brownfields sites.*

- • *Encourage and support the involvement of non-traditional stakeholders (such as community-based organizations) in government processes, such as zoning issues.*

- • *Identify the real costs of Greenfields development.*

III. Public and Private Sector Partnerships

8. Community/Private Sector Partnerships:

At the root of many problems confronting urban/Brownfields communities are massive economic shifts that have marked the past two decades. New approaches towards building partnerships between decaying inner city communities and newer suburban are a vital necessity. Decay in both physical and social infrastructure pose great obstacles to reinvestment and revitalization. Urban revitalization/Brownfields programs must form partnerships with groups beyond the traditional Brownfields stakeholder groups to include community based organizations, youth groups, faith groups, labor groups, civil rights groups, public health groups, and philanthropy. Government agencies and societal institutions must not view communities as merely an assortment of needs but as a collection of assets which can be built upon.

- *Institute a Brownfields grant program which provides funds directly to community groups in partnership with locally based non-governmental institutions.*

- *Convene a National Urban Revitalization/Brownfields Summit Meeting of all stakeholders working on or affected by Brownfields projects as an opportunity to bring together all parties to discuss critical issues, craft unified strategies, and determine actions for follow-up.*

9. Local, State, Tribal, and Territorial Government:

Local, state, tribal, and territorial governments increasingly recognize the importance of addressing contaminated properties and Brownfields issues. Mature communities, both urban and rural, are confronting several generations of Brownfields. At the same time, municipalities lack the capacity and resources to develop effective urban revitalization/Brownfields programs. Tribal and territorial governments have often overlooked special issues such as sovereignty and infrastructure. States will have key roles because they will provide regulatory oversight for voluntary cleanup. Improved communications to better understand differing roles and needs is critical, as is building the capacity of local communities to work with each level of government.

- *Improve communications and coordination between and among multiple levels of government to enable an integrated approach to Brownfields as part of overall community revitalization efforts.*

- *Provide training on environmental justice and Brownfields for local, state, tribal and territorial governments.*

- *Develop a Brownfields grant program specifically designed to meet the special needs of Native American Tribes and U.S. Territories.*

10. Federal Interagency Cooperation, Programmatic Integration, and Government Reinvention:

The original and most enduring proponents of government reinvention are community residents engaged in overcoming systemic impediments to locally based solutions. The heart and soul of an authentic government reinvention process must be based upon vibrant and coherent community-based visions of healthy and sustainable communities. There already exists many federal policy and program initiatives which lend themselves to viable integrative strategies. In seeking to address a set of placed-based, multi-faceted, and cross-cutting set of issues, urban revitalization/Brownfields efforts provide unique opportunities for programmatic integration and government reinvention.

- • *Establish an interagency task force on Urban Revitalization/Brownfields, either through the Interagency Working Group on Environmental Justice or some other appropriate mechanism, to ensure programmatic coordination and integration.*

- • *Provide opportunities for communities to systematically engage EPA and other federal around ways in which federal programs around ways by which they can coordinate programs, pool resources and tap expertise.*

Conclusion

The urban revitalization/Brownfields debate reveals issues of civilizational dimensions. As we look to the 21st century, what endeavor could possibly be more eminently worthy and necessary; more obviously logical and deserving of our national attention, expertise, and resources; or more meaningful and spiritually nourishing than that of revitalizing America's urban areas and ensuring healthy and sustainable communities, both urban and rural? A challenge so great as this cannot be met with compelling visions of what constitutes healthy and sustainable communities. We have found that such visions already exist in highly coherent and vibrant ways within many communities across the nation.

The Nation is locked within the throes of a set of transitions which are demographic, economic, environmental, technological, social, cultural, linguistic, generational, and indeed spiritual in nature. Urban revitalization and Brownfields offer an opportunity to shape new policy, programs, partnerships, and pilot projects which rise to the challenge of the cross-cutting issues raised in this report. The Subcommittee continues to pose these questions:

- Can this process begin to set a direction capable of crystallizing a unifying and cross-cutting vision within the federal government to serve as an anchor for the mobilization of society's resources--both public and private?

- Can the restoration of the physical environment in America's cities become the anchoring point for economic, social, cultural, and spiritual renewal and thus provide the basis for a embarking upon a new and ennobling national mission?

These questions form the guiding elements for envisioning the next phase of urban revitalization/Brownfields strategies. The NEJAC Subcommittee felt the need to identify priorities for the next two to four years from the above recommendations. The Subcommittee recognized that the Brownfields Initiative has achieve broad-based support because it linked two critical areas, i.e., environmental cleanup with job creation. Over the past year, the Subcommittee has worked to stimulate dialogue on ensuring the following issue linkages:

- • Environmental cleanup with job creation
- • Federal facilities cleanup and restoration with urban revitalization/Brownfields
- • Urban revitalization/Brownfields with transportation, regional land use, and the Department of Transportation's "Livable Communities" Initiative
- • Urban revitalization/Brownfields, public health, and community-based planning

We believe that a maturing discussion on the above issues will take place over the next year and provide the catalyst for a unified federal approach towards coalescing a common urban revitalization strategy across all federal agencies. Several other priorities must take place over the next two to four years:

• • Establish an interagency urban revitalization/Brownfields task force, either through the Federal Interagency Working Group on Environmental Justice or other appropriate mechanisms;

• • Convene a National Urban Revitalization/Brownfields Summit (this should be portrayed as a •national revival• for the cities);

• • Support the establishment of a National Urban Revitalization/Brownfields Training Institute to develop and train in achieving healthy and sustainable communities;

• • Convene a dialogue between community groups and developers/investors to achieve a common framework for decision making and working partnerships;

• • Ensure support for worker training programs and establish mechanisms for better coordination;

• • Establish special grant programs in areas of technical assistance to communities, small grants for community-based advocacy and training, and a tribal and territorial Brownfields grant program

• • Establish new partnerships above and beyond traditional urban revitalization/Brownfields stakeholders to include community-based organizations, youth groups, faith groups, labor groups, civil rights groups, public health groups, and philanthropic organizations.

If the Brownfields issue is nothing else, it was an opportunity for community groups to engage government, developers, and other stakeholders around their vision of what healthy and sustainable communities are. The stakes cannot be greater. EPA must begin to think about a new framework which will address the issues raised through the Public Dialogues on Urban Revitalization and Brownfields. The hallmark of that process must be informed and empowered community involvement. Likewise, all agencies in the federal government should consider these cross-cutting issues and begin to shape coordinated and integrative strategies.

The NEJAC Subcommittee on Waste and Facility Siting believes that a process has been started by which environmental justice advocates and impacted communities have changed the operative definition of the term "Brownfields." This already has translated into some significant changes in the way in which EPA implements the Brownfields Initiative. We hope to engage a process which ultimately will coalesce a new type of environmental and social policy capable of meeting the challenges of revitalizing urban America and restoring ecological balance to the nation. This was our intent. Anything less would have amounted to a failure of leadership, a breaking of faith with communities, and acquiescence to business as usual.

ENVIRONMENTAL JUSTICE, URBAN REVITALIZATION, AND BROWNFIELDS:

THE SEARCH FOR AUTHENTIC SIGNS OF HOPE

*The vision of environmental justice is the development of a holistic, bottom-up, community-based, multi-issue, cross-cutting, and integrative, and unifying paradigm for achieving healthy and sustainable communities--both urban and rural. In the context of ecological peril, economic dysfunction, infrastructure decay, racial polarization, social turmoil, cultural disorientation, and spiritual malaise which grips urban America at the end of the 20th century, environmental justice is indeed a much needed breath of fresh air. Tragically, many positive developments have been rendered invisible behind the curtain of a sensationalism-oriented mass media. However, there is no denying that great resilience exists in the economic, cultural, and spiritual life of America's communities. There are many stellar accomplishments, entrepreneurial successes, and significant victories--both big and small. Hence, an abiding goal of the Public Dialogues on Urban Revitalization and Brownfields was the **constant search for authentic signs of hope**.*

INTRODUCTION

In 1995, the National Environmental Justice Advisory Council (NEJAC) Waste and Facility Siting Subcommittee and the U.S. Environmental Protection Agency (EPA) co-sponsored a series of public hearings entitled "Public Dialogues on Urban Revitalization and Brownfields: Envisioning Healthy and Sustainable Communities." NEJAC is the formal advisory committee convened by EPA to provide advice on issues of environmental justice. It consists of grassroots leaders from impacted communities, environmental justice scholars and advocates, and representatives from a broad range of stakeholder groups.

The NEJAC Waste and Facility Siting Subcommittee (hereafter referred to as the Subcommittee) is sponsored by EPA's Office of Solid Waste and Emergency Response (OSWER). OSWER was the first program office within the federal government to develop a comprehensive environmental justice strategy. Under the leadership of Assistant Administrator Elliot P. Laws, OSWER began the process of developing its environmental justice strategy prior to the signing by President Clinton of Executive Order 12898.[1]

Five Public Dialogues were held in Boston, Massachusetts; Philadelphia, Pennsylvania; Detroit, Michigan; Oakland, California; and Atlanta, Georgia. They were intended to provide, for the first time, an opportunity for environmental justice advocates and residents of impacted communities to **systematically contribute input** regarding issues related to EPA's Brownfields Economic Redevelopment Initiative. Over 500 persons from community groups, government agencies, faith

> ### National Environmental Justice Advisory Council (NEJAC)
>
> NEJAC is a federal advisory committee that was established on September 30, 1993 to provide independent advice, consultation, and recommendations to the EPA Administrator. Its members represent diverse stakeholder groups, including academia, industry, community groups, various non-governmental organizations, state and local governments, tribal organizations, and environmental organizations.
>
> In 1994 and 1995, NEJAC consisted of four subcommittees: Health and Research, Enforcement, Public Participation and Accountability, and Waste and Facility Siting. In December 1995, two new subcommittees--International and Indigenous Peoples) were established. NEJAC is chaired by Mr. Richard Moore, Southwest Network for Environmental and Economic Justice.

groups, labor organizations, philanthropies, universities, banks, businesses, and other institutions participated in a "systematic attempt to stimulate a new and vigorous public discourse about developing strategies, partnerships, models, and projects for ensuring healthy and sustainable communities in America's urban centers and their importance to the nation's environmental and economic future." Representatives from 15 federal agencies, as well as state and local governments, participated in the meetings.

The Public Dialogues sought to provide an opportunity for environmental justice advocates and community-based groups in impacted areas (1) to become a visible and meaningful part of an already existing national discourse on issues related to Brownfields hazardous site cleanup and economic redevelopment, (2) to reshape in substantive ways the development of EPA's Brownfields Initiative, and (3) add a new dimension to public policy discourse on Brownfields and urban redevelopment. At the point that the Brownfields issue came to NEJAC's attention, most issues to be addressed, such as liability issues, seemed to be "developer-driven." Most, if not all, public policy discussion about Brownfields was shaped by a desire to effect changes in legislation, regulatory standards, and liability provisions to meet the concerns of prospective investors and developers. Most people in potentially impacted communities had never heard the term "Brownfields."[2] NEJAC found that given the opportunity to define the issues surrounding Brownfields, these communities would do so in very different ways.

The Public Dialogues sought to be community-driven in terms of planning, preparation, structure, and execution. They proceeded from the premise that a strong sense of collective concerns and aspirations already existed within many communities. These comprise highly coherent and compelling visions of healthy and sustainable communities. Some communities have engaged in highly sophisticated community-based planning and visioning processes.

The Public Dialogues were structured into two tiers. First, communities articulated their concerns about the Brownfields initiative and their visions for achieving healthy and sustainable communities. Second, representatives of government agencies, as well as key social institutions such as labor, faith groups, universities, philanthropies, and business organizations, were asked to address the role they can play in helping to make the community's vision a reality. By structuring the Public Dialogues to model new forms of public participation, the

---

Members of the
WASTE AND FACILITY SITING
SUBCOMMITTEE

Mr. Charles Lee, Chair
Ms. Jan Young, DFO

Ms. Dollie Burwell
Ms. Sue Briggum
Ms. Teresa Cordova
Mr. Donald Elisburg
Mr. Michael Guererro
Mr. Tom Goldtooth
Mr. David Hahn-Baker
Ms. Lillian Kawasaki
Mr. Tom Kennedy
Mr. Scott Morrison
Mr. Jon Sesso
Mr. Lenny Siegel
Ms. Connie Tucker
Ms. Nathalie Walker

Interagency Participation

Among the Federal agencies present at the Public Dialogues were:

•• U.S. Environmental Protection Agency
•• U.S. Department of Transportation
•• U.S. Department of Housing and Urban Development
•• U.S. Department of Defense
•• U.S. Department of Energy
•• U.S. Department of Health and Human Services
•• U.S. Department of Justice
•• U.S. Department of Labor
•• U.S. Department of Interior
•• U.S. Department of Agriculture
•• Centers for Disease Control and Prevention
•• National Institute of Environmental Health Sciences
•• Economic Development Administration
•• U.S. Forestry Service
•• National Institute for Occupational Safety and Health

Subcommittee was intent on putting the discourse about Brownfields issues into a context that the community both defines and articulates.

The Public Dialogues abide by the basic environmental justice tenet that *"people must speak for themselves*."[3] Therefore, in an effort to uphold the integrity of the testimony presented, the Subcommittee believes that to the degree possible, any resulting report would retain the voice of the speakers. To reduce the community presentations to the language of "techno-speak" effectively would have sanitized their message, rendered them devoid of conviction, and destroyed their interest. This would do disservice to community members who went to great efforts to participate. Perhaps more than any other single factor, the question of whose language is used determines whether or not a process is truly community-driven. To capture the community message therefore, community presentations are quoted extensively throughout this report. Although the report is long, the Subcommittee strongly urges readers to respect the community members by taking the time to seriously read their statements. This is necessary to work towards bridging the huge disconnect now existing between the public, government bureaucracy, and the decision-making process. In many ways, this report is also a collection of stories and perspectives. As such, it builds upon a rich oral tradition in communities and among peoples of color.

APPLICATION OF THE
NEJAC PUBLIC PARTICIPATION MODEL

The planning and implementation of the *Public Dialogues on Urban Revitalization and Brownfields* attempted to "model" new forms of public participation by incorporating key elements of the Public Participation Model developed in October 1994 by the NEJAC Public Participation and Accountability Subcommittee. These elements included:

•• Up-front community involvement in planning, preparation, and definition of issues

•• Two-way, focused interactive dialogue on a given set of issues

•• Fact-finding meetings held in communities other than Washington, D.C.

•• Recognition of local community history which includes language, culture, and experience

•• Exploration of ways to make use of non-governmental vehicles for public participation, such as NEJAC

•• Finding new ways of building partnerships between communities, government, and other stakeholders

•• A body of information and contacts left within communities

•• Development of models which can be replicated

•• Most importantly, an explicitly stated intention of the host agency to demonstrate that it listened to the community

---

BACKGROUND

EPA defines Brownfields as "abandoned, idled, or under-used industrial and commercial facilities where expansion or redevelopment is complicated by real or perceived environmental contamination." In January 1995, Administrator Carol Browner announced that EPA will fund 50 pilot projects across the country as part of its Brownfields Economic Redevelopment Initiative.

The EPA Brownfields Economic Redevelopment Initiative is a program which seeks to find ways to remove barriers to the return to beneficial reuse of properties whose redevelopment is complicated by environmental contamination--whether real or perceived. EPA's expressed hope is that these sites can become a source of jobs and help in restoring depleted tax bases. The U.S. General Accounting Office has estimated that such sites could number as many 450,000 across the country, including abandoned and/or underutilized warehouses, gas stations, and factories. For example, Eugenio Maria de Hostos Community College houses 5,500 students and provides a major institutional anchor for the South Bronx, New York. It was founded during the 1960's in an abandoned tire factory. Today, the facility would be classified as a successfully redeveloped Brownfields site. In Oakland, California, Preservation Park--a renovated development which is home to several non-profit organizations--stands as a symbol of hope and renewal in the midst of urban deterioration. It too would be classified as a successfully redeveloped Brownfields site.

The Subcommittee offered substantial input to the finalization of the OSWER *Environmental Justice Action Agenda*, published in June 1995. Recognizing OSWER's environmental justice strategy as a "living document," the Subcommittee adopted a Ten-Point Implementation Framework for OSWER's action agenda. Many of these implementation points are directly relevant to the Subcommittee's approach to its work around EPA's Brownfields action agenda. In its report to the NEJAC at the meeting held October 27, 1994 in Dulles, Virginia, the Subcommittee stated that:

> *"[it] recognizes the cross-cutting nature of environmental justice and therefore sees the necessary limitations of program-specific, or even agency-specific, environmental justice strategies. However, environmental justice will be rendered meaningless if it is not actively integrated into all EPA programs and other agencies within the federal government. The Subcommittee set forth the challenge of attempting to offer a vision for an environmental protection policy in the 21st century--especially as it relates to major societal issues of our times. This compels a thoughtful critique of traditional policy constructs and program demarcations. Hence, the Subcommittee sees great value in effective usage of the Presidential Executive Order 12898 on environmental justice. Recognizing OSWER's unique position as the first program office to develop such a strategy, the Subcommittee urges OSWER to serve as a catalyst for such integration."*

The following points, outlined in the Framework, are directly relevant to the Brownfields Initiative:

• • Comprehensive and interactive approaches to communications, outreach and public participation is a *hub* of environmental justice strategy implementation.

• • Ensuring culturally diverse and community-driven training of agency personnel is critical to the agency's ability to serve all groups in an increasingly multiracial and multicultural society.

• • Efforts must continue to build institutional infrastructure [4] for achieving environmental justice within OSWER and other related EPA programs; other federal agency programs; partnerships with state, local and tribal governments, community groups, and other stakeholders.

•• An integrative Environmental Justice Model Demonstration Program approach should be used as the *template* for project implementation.

Concerns were raised by members of the public about the Brownfields Initiative, i.e., whether or not the Brownfields issue was a "smoke screen" for gutting cleanup standards, environmental regulations, and liability safeguards. Over the past three years, substantial national momentum had been building related to the Brownfields concept. For example, in 1995 the U.S. Conference of Mayors designated Brownfields as its No. 1 environmental priority. To a large extent, public policy related to the Brownfields issue revolved around removing barriers to real estate and investment transactions at sites where there exist toxic contamination concerns--real or perceived.

From the point of view of the Subcommittee and environmental justice advocates, EPA had received virtually no meaningful input from environmental justice advocates or residents from impacted communities about the Brownfields initiative. By 1994, EPA had initiated an environmental justice outreach and minority worker training program at the Cuyahoga County Community College in Cleveland, Ohio, which is linked to the Brownfields Pilot in Cuyahoga County.

> **An Integrative Environmental Justice Model Demonstration Approach**
>
> The Environmental Justice/Community Issues Working Group of the National Advisory Council on Environmental Policy and Technology (NACEPT) Superfund Evaluation Committee (1993) originally submitted to EPA a list of key elements. The list included integration of:
>
> • • formulation of policy and regulatory frameworks
> • • development of analytical tools, indicators, and protocols for environmental justice
> • • community-wide, multi-media, targeted geographic initiatives
> • • public health concerns of impacted communities and multiple, cumulative and synergistic risk
> • • built-in mechanisms for community participation and empowerment
> • • federal interagency cooperation
> • • economic redevelopment and sustainable community
> • • enhancement of community user-friendly pollution prevention and technology diffusion programs
> • • strategies for stakeholder involvement including labor, business, non-profit, philanthropic, and other institutional partners
> • • ongoing evaluation, coordination and integration of existing pilots and programs

However, in light of the breadth of the Brownfields issue, the Subcommittee clearly felt the effort did not accomplish environment justice; as the subcommittee noted, •EPA•s Brownfields locomotive left the station without a major group of passengers.• The Subcommittee's objectives in sponsoring the Public Dialogues were to achieve a meaningful role by environmental justice advocates and residents from potentially-impacted communities, and to initiate dialogue among stakeholder groups on addressing community goals.

At the same time, there was hope that the Brownfields Initiative could provide an opportunity to:

• • stem the ecologically untenable, environmentally damaging, socially costly, and racially divisive phenomenon of urban sprawl, displacement of residents through gentrification, and Greenfields development

• • provide focus to a problem which by its very nature is inextricably linked to environmental justice, for example, the physical deterioration of the nation's urban areas

• • allow communities to offer their vision of what redevelopment should look like

• • apply environmental justice principles to the development of a new generation of environmental policy capable of meeting complex challenges such as Brownfields and the existence of a severe crisis in urban America

• • bring greater awareness and opportunities for building partnerships between EPA, communities and other stakeholders.

NATIONAL ENVIRONMENTAL JUSTICE ADVISORY COUNCIL
Resolution on Environmental Justice and Urban Revitalization
Crystal City, Virginia
July 25-26, 1995

WHEREAS the nation confronts no more worthy, necessary, and compelling challenge than that of addressing the existence of a severe crisis in America's urban centers and the need for a new national commitment to urban revitalization;

WHEREAS the vision of environmental justice is the development of a holistic, bottoms-up, community-based, multi-faceted, cross-cutting, and integrative paradigm for achieving healthy and sustainable communities, both urban and rural;

WHEREAS the urban eco-system at the end of the twentieth century is comprised of four environments, i.e., the natural, built, social, and cultural/spiritual environments;

WHEREAS environmental justice is uniquely equipped to provide the visions, the frameworks, and the tools capable of meeting this great national challenge;

WHEREAS the urban crisis is fundamentally an ecological one, rooted in among other things the racial makeup of the structure of American cities; and

WHEREAS revitalizing urban America requires a unified and integrated strategy on the part of all federal agencies, in the spirit of a community-driven government reinvention process.

THEREFORE SO BE IT RESOLVED that the National Environmental Justice Advisory Council requests the Administrator of the U.S. Environmental Protection Agency to undertake the following action items:

• • Provide leadership in stimulating a new and vigorous national public discourse over the compelling need to develop strategies for ensuring healthy and sustainable communities in America's urban centers and their importance to the nation's environmental and economic future.

• • Perform a review of all EPA programs, both national and regional, to ensure the development of innovative, effective, equitable, and lasting strategies, partnerships, models, and pilot projects for achieving healthy and sustainable urban communities.

• • Request that the development of one unified, integrated, and cross-cutting national strategy to address issues of urban revitalization and the development of healthy and sustainable urban communities be made a priority agenda item for the implementation of Executive Order 12898 and the work of the Federal Interagency Working Group on Environmental Justice.

As a result of the Public Dialogues, the National Environmental Justice Advisory Council adopted at its July 25-26, 1995 meeting in Crystal City, Virginia, a resolution entitled "Environmental Justice and Urban Revitalization."

KEY ISSUES IN THE BROWNFIELDS DEBATE

The concept of "Brownfields" emerged as a natural outgrowth of groups and individuals seeking to reverse the tide of urban decay. One impediment which readily presented itself to such groups, including those seeking to build low-income housing for the homeless, was the environmental liability issues associated with abandoned commercial and industrial properties. Such properties are abundantly located in virtually every "other side of the tracks" community in America's urban areas. The Northeast/Midwest Institute[5] coined the term "Brownfields" to describe this phenomenon. While not all Brownfields are located in urban areas, the environmental policy and sociological context of the Brownfields problem is decidedly urban in character.

In a narrow sense, EPA's Brownfields Initiative refers to a specific agency effort focusing on finding ways to remove items which are viewed as obstacles to investment by prospective lenders and developers. Many concerns over the specific elements of that program, including the need for meaningful community involvement, environmental health considerations, job creation and training, federal interagency cooperation, public/private partnerships, and others began to surface. In order to fully address these important issues, they must be considered within a larger context.

> *"[South Central Los Angeles] is a community characterized by tons and tons of vacant lots, some of them left as a result of the 1992 rebellion. Others have existed for 20 and 30 years. My community also is characterized by auto shops, paint shops, plating companies, radiator companies, and others--some of which are unpermitted uses within our residential community. Our community suffers one of the highest incidence of asthma throughout California. It sits next to the largest industrial base in this country called the Alameda Corridor. The neighborhood has pretty much been neglected by the city of Los Angeles in terms of street repairs, storm drainage cleaning, and so forth.*
>
> *"We see the Brownfields Initiative as a real opportunity to change some of what exists in our community. A lot of sites have been left behind by owners who could not free up or sell land because of contamination--whether they were once gas stations or whatever. So we see ourselves losing a lot of potential for good, clean, safe, and sound development.*
>
> *"We also have concerns about some Brownfields initiatives. Even when one is something we tend to like, we feel the prospective purchaser agreements must have more teeth and accountability [to the community]. We feel strongly that community participation must be involved. We would never like to see something cleaned up and then a liquor store put in my community. We must have a say on the front-end as to what kind of development follows cleanup.*
>
> *"In terms of jobs and job training, people in my community have strong concerns about who benefits from job [opportunities]. There is justifiably much discussion about military conversion, aerospace conversion, and conversion jobs. But how does the community where people have a lack of skills get involved in the discussion? We want to be able to bring the nonworking and underemployed into the discussion. These are some of the concerns we would like to see addressed."*
>
> Robin Canon
> Concerned Citizens of South Central Los Angeles
> Oakland, CA, Public Dialogue

In a larger sense, the Brownfields issue propelled to national prominence the issues related to **"Brownfields versus Greenfields"** development. If society cannot find ways of revitalizing urban areas, development necessarily encroaches more and more on the nonrenewable resource of pristine natural space. The emergence of the Brownfields issue signals recognition of the ecologically untenable nature of "Greenfields" development or urban sprawl. A coalition which includes Bank of America, Greenbelt Alliance, Low-Income Housing Fund, and the Resources Agency of California, recently published *Beyond Sprawl: New Patterns of Growth to Fit the New California*. It concluded that the "acceleration of sprawl has surfaced enormous social, environmental, and economic costs, which until now have been hidden, ignored, or quietly borne by society. The burden of these costs is becoming very clear. Businesses suffer from higher costs, a loss in worker productivity, and underutilized investments in older communities."[6]

The Brownfields issue is yet another aspect of an intensifying set of systemic problems related to residential segregation, disinvestment of inner-city areas, urban sprawl, degradation of the urban environment, and the polarization between urban and non-urban communities along lines of age, life style, race, socioeconomic status, and other spatially-related social divisions. These are endemic to a severe crisis--environmentally, economically, socially, culturally, and otherwise--in urban America. Environmental justice encompasses very clearly the inextricable linkage between these issues. The Subcommittee emphatically asserts that all stakeholder groups must recognize that the inescapable context for discussion of the Brownfields issue is environmental justice and urban revitalization.

The following summarizes some of these pressing issues related to urban revitalization, Brownfields, and the achievement of truly healthy and sustainable communities--both urban and rural. The Subcommittee proceeds from the recognition that one of the nation's most pressing environmental problems is the state of its cities. This crisis is fundamentally an ecological one--in both the natural and the human sense.[7] While one may choose to deny their existence, it is increasingly evident that they cannot be ignored.

I.   *Understanding the Nature of the Urban Environment*

Based on environmental justice principles, the Subcommittee defines environment as *"the place where we live, where we work, and where we play."*[8] This necessitates recognition of an urban ecosystem as consisting of four environments: natural, built, social, and cultural/spiritual. All four must be addressed in order to achieve healthy and sustainable communities. Hence, the debate over cleanup standards, environmental regulations, and liability safeguards must proceed from a realistic understanding of the environmental health and safety characteristics of the urban environment. The urban ecosystem shows clearly the relationship of these four environments, and the importance of the fourth environment--Cultural/Spiritual--to provide an understanding of shared values to achieve healthy environments and sustainable communities.

The characteristics of the urban environment include: (1) an oversaturation of communities with multiple sources of environmental pollution in highly congested spaces, (2) the co-existence of residential and industrial sites as a result of imprudent land use decisions, (3) a lack of documentation of most environmental health risks in urban communities, (4) the existence of as yet not understood effects of multiple, cumulative, and synergistic risks, (5) the absence of a comprehensive environmental enforcement and compliance activity which results, for some communities, in a virtual non-existence of such activity, (6) the lack of health services and adequate information on environmental risks, (7) the severe decay in the institutional infrastructure, and (8) a high degree of social alienation and decay caused by living in degraded physical environments.

The profusion of abandoned and/or contaminated industrial and commercial sites is a legacy of industrialization and patterns of growth which foster social decay by treating land, natural resources, communities, and populations as expendable and disposable commodities. Any redevelopment strategy must be thoroughly examined to ascertain its guiding vision and potential pitfalls. It must not be the vehicle for development of yet another generation of hazardous sites. It must not be the instrument of ecologically-unsustainable or socially-unjust development.

II.   *The Ecological Importance of Urban Areas*

In choosing to concentrate on urban revitalization as a major focus, the Subcommittee underscores the societal and ecological importance of cities. Besides being the centers of economic, technological, educational, and cultural activity in an increasingly multiracial United States, urban environments pose vastly important opportunities for advancing human understanding of environmental protection needs for the 21st century. Solving these questions will have enormous implications for habitat development not only for the United States but also a shrinking and increasingly interdependent world.

> *"We are looking at environmental justice in a regional context. It is a vision of making links between different communities across the region with common perspectives of how we look at social issues as well as environmental issues. Based upon that, we seek to develop strategies that help to address the polarization between suburban and inner city areas. Working on Brownfields gives us an opportunity to make this tangible."*
>
> Carl Anthony
> Urban Habitat Program
> Oakland, CA, Public Dialogue

The paradox that faces us at the end of the 20th century is that urban areas are ecologically the most efficient forms of human spatial organization, while at the same time they are among the most polluted. Urban areas present pressing challenges on the cutting edge of environmental protection and sustainable development, including such challenges as multiple, cumulative, and synergistic risks; pollution prevention; creation of environmentally-related jobs; development of "green," non-polluting, and environmentally restorative urban development; and building of mass transit and ecologically-beneficial infrastructures; as well as a host of other issues.

Given the massive scale of human development, these are challenges the Nation cannot afford to ignore. Urban environmental issues must be addressed from the perspective of their natural ecosystems (for example, water sheds, air sheds, etc.) and their social ecosystems (for example, neighborhoods, metropolitan areas, regions, etc). As exemplified by the •Brownfields redevelopment versus Greenfields development• debate, the course of development in urban areas has enormous impacts for the past, present, and future ecological integrity of rural areas.

The Subcommittee believes that an affirmative commitment to urban revitalization will lead to a necessary evaluation of traditional social policy and value systems. At this point, the nation lacks the tools to measure the true costs--economic, environmental, cultural, social, and spiritual--of the untenable and unsustainable treatment of goods, communities, and population as expendable and disposable commodities. The Subcommittee attests to a critical need for the nation to embrace the concepts of reuse, recycling, renewal, revitalization, and rebirth. The ecological crisis exemplified by the state of the urban environment offers such an opportunity.

III.   *Reframing the Urban/Rural Dichotomy*

One context for understanding the Brownfields issue is the issue of urbanization. Urbanization refers to the formation, growth, and transformation of human communities as centers of industrial, commercial, social, and cultural activity. From an ecological perspective, this affects both urban and rural areas in an interdependent manner. A multiplicity of development issues such as residential patterns, displacement throught gentrification, transportation policy, the flow of capital, and others profoundly affect patterns of growth. Environmental justice recognizes the inextricable linkages between these as economic, environmental, cultural, and social issues.

Twentieth century human development is characterized by the interrelated twin phenomena of industrialization and urbanization. The emergence of centers of industrial activity always gave rise to a corresponding appearance of

Industrialization and Urbanization

Nothing better illustrates the severity of the twin phenomena of industrialization and urbanization than Richard Monastersky's 1994 article in *Science News*, entitled "Earthmovers: Humans take their place alongside wind, water, and ice" (Vol. 146, Dec. 24 & 31, 1994, pp. 432-433).

According to the article, studies suggest that human activity, as of 1994, now transforms the earth's surface at a rate that exceeds natural geological processes. It is estimated that homo sapiens move an average of seven tons of earth a year for every man, woman, and child on the planet.

proximate population centers. Historically, society has been deficient in its attention to issues surrounding such "spontaneously" developing communities.[9] Urbanization refers not merely to events in the Northern "rust-belt" cities but also to the phenomenon that is taking place along the U.S.-Mexico border in the form of a mindless urban sprawl called "colonias."

The Subcommittee argues that only through an affirmative declaration of the importance of the urban environment can the Nation begin to bridge the dichotomy between urban and rural areas. We need to develop models which unify rather than pit urban versus non-urban concerns. The urban sprawl issue forces us to envision new ecological relationships which are metropolitan, regional, national, and global. By its very nature, the Brownfields issue forces us to look at an entire community as we try to balance environmental concerns and economic possibilities. In many cases, it becomes an ideal vehicle for envisioning the future in new ways.

In addition, even though this report focuses primarily on urban revitalization/Brownfields issues, the NEJAC Subcommittee is mindful that Brownfields issue exist in rural areas. Brownfields issues are also matters of great concern on Native American lands and in the U.S. territories, most of which is rural in nature. Nonetheless, development patterns have reached the point where urbanization has direct economic, environmental, social, and ecological consequences for rural lands. All references to Indigenous peoples, Native Americans, and Tribes includes American Indians and Alaskan Natives.

IV.   *Confronting the Issue of Race and Class*

Embedded into America's industrial legacy are a host of issues related to race and class. The nation cannot ignore the very obvious and central place that issues of race occupy in the daily lives of all its citizens. There exists a "great racial divide" in American society. This divide is manifest through our treatment of issues related to urban America.

Not more than six months after the historic First National People of Color Environmental Leadership Summit held in 1991, the largest urban disturbance in American history took place in South Central Los Angeles. Events in Los Angeles raised the question of how long the "quiet riots"[10] (a phrase drawn from the title of a 20-year retrospective to the 1968 Kerner Commission Report) in America's central cities will continue to remain unheard. Issues at the heart of these "quiet riots" are inextricably linked to environmental justice and Brownfields, such as residential segregation, economic disinvestment, environmental pollution, inaccessibility to health care, educational disadvantage, lack of employment opportunity, and the inextricable link between living in degraded physical environments, alienation, and destructive violence.

All policy makers must find every opportunity to forthrightly confront issues of race and class in American society. Not to do so is shortsighted for the following reasons: (1) Race is a matter at the heart of many issues related to urban America and we as a nation must learn how to talk about it in constructive ways; (2) Healthy and sustainable communities cannot be achieved without fully understanding how racism seriously devalues communities; and (3) American society in the 21st century will be increasingly multiracial and multicultural. Dramatic demographic shifts are taking place. The choices we make today will decide whether or not 21st-century America will witness a social turmoil or a multiracial and multicultural renaissance where the gifts of all peoples can flourish.[11] It is imperative that guidance be provided--particularly to our youth who will inherit the consequences of choices we make today--to reinforce a sense of purpose for a common future and to focus them towards a goal of narrowing and eliminating racial divisions.

V.   *Urban Revitalization and Community-Driven Models of Redevelopment*

"Urban revitalization" is very different from "urban redevelopment." The two concepts are not synonymous and should not be confused with each other. Urban revitalization is a bottom-up process. It proceeds from a community-based vision of its needs and aspirations and seeks to build capacity, build partnerships, and mobilize resources to make the vision a reality. Revitalization, as we define it, does not lead to displacement of communities through gentrification that often results from redevelopment policies. Governments must not simply view communities as an assortment of problems but also as a collection of assets. Social scientists and practitioners have already compiled methodologies to apply community planning models.

There must be opportunities for full articulation of the importance of public participation in Brownfields issue. While public participation is cross-cutting in nature, its meaning is shaped within the context of concrete issues. It is not merely a set of mechanical prescriptions but a process of bottom-up engagement that is "living." With regards to Brownfields and the future of urban America, Public Dialogue participants were emphatic that *"without meaningful community involvement, urban revitalization simply becomes urban redevelopment."*

John Kretzmann and John L. McKnight summarized the key steps in applying community planning models in their book, *Building Communities from the Inside Out: A Path Toward Finding and Mobilizing A Community's Assets*:

•• Mapping completely the capacities and assets of individuals, citizens' associations, and local institutions
•• Building relationships among local assets for mutually beneficial problem-solving within the community
•• Mobilizing the community's assets fully for economic development and information sharing purposes
•• Convening as broadly representative a group as possible for the purposes of building a community vision and plan
•• Leveraging activities, investments and resources from outside the community to support asset-based, locally-defined development.

VI.   Community Mapping and Community-Based Environmental Protection

Mapping offers us an entirely new way of looking at and thinking about the world. A principal tenet of community-based planning is the thesis that a community which has a strong sense of itself is capable of being more self-defined, self-directed, and self-controlled, and thus more capable of shaping its own future.[12]

There appears to be an ever-expanding number of community groups who are expressing an interest in mapping one's own community. These include organizations concerned about environmental justice, environmental and public health, community planning and development, and other issues related to achieving healthy and sustainable communities. This "spontaneous" development is a matter of no small consequence. Recent projects to incorporate community mapping as an important element include the Asian Pacific Environmental Network (Laotian girls mapping their Richmond, California neighborhood); Tucsonians for a Clean Environment (development in south Tucson, Arizona); worker training projects such as Southwest Network for Environmental and Economic Justice, Asian Pacific Environmental Network, University of California/Berkeley, and the University of Massachusetts/Lowell;

LAND VIEW II
A Community Mapping Tool

LAND VIEW II--an electronic atlas with the ability to do thematic mapping--is a unique electronic tool which can be the hub of a virtual revolution in community mapping. As described by EPA, LAND VIEW II is an innovative community right-to-know software tool. In the form of an electronic atlas, published on CD-ROM discs, LAND VIEW can be used on standard personal computers. While LAND VIEW lends itself to a myriad of applications, its greatest significance lies in its useability and adaptability by communities.

LAND VIEW II is the product of a collaboration among EPA, the Bureau of the Census, and the National Oceanic and Atmospheric Administration (NOAA). As the product of a multi-agency cooperative effort that was developed with substantial community input, LAND VIEW II bespeaks of what government should be doing in terms of providing tools that can empower the public.

The Subcommittee incorporated demonstrations of LAND VIEW II as a major part of the Public Dialogues. The universally positive reception by the communities underscored the Subcommittee's belief that mapping can be a highly empowering scoping, documenting, and planning tool. Such tools give a community the ability to visualize and "know" itself.

and the Environmental Health Coalition, (chemical hazards in mixed-use Barrio Logan community in San Diego, California).[13]   One of the most powerful elements of the landmark United Church of Christ Commission for Racial Justice report *Toxic Wastes and Race in the United States*[14] was its maps. Virtually every proposal on empowerment zones and Brownfields uses mapping.

Projects with more resources such as the Hunter College/Greenpoint-Williamsburg Environmental Benefits Program have done true computer-based GIS projects. Eugenio Maria de Hostos Community College in the South Bronx is undertaking a major community-university partnership project in this area. The San Francisco-based Urban Habitat Program has done mapping of military toxic waste sites and the impact of defense base closures in East Bay Flatlands areas.[15] Several EPA regional offices also have undertaken GIS studies. For example, EPA Region III is utilizing GIS in Chester, Pennsylvania and at the Portsmouth, Virginia Superfund site. In varying degrees of complexity, these projects offer readily applicable tools for conducting community mapping projects.

Exciting new tools exist for communities to participate in conducting environmental inventories and environmental mapping. These include right-to-know information, electronic mapping systems like LandView II, more sophisticated geographic information systems (GIS), and others.   It is critical that these tools be made available to communities. Beside its implications for community-based planning, community mapping will be critical to addressing issues of multiple, cumulative, and synergistic risk. By fully engaging the community, these tools provide a way to begin addressing data gap problems in oversaturated urban communities where virtually none of the environmental health risks have yet to be documented. Thus, community mapping provides a key link to making progress on issues such as cumulative risk and the concept of establishing the "baseline aggregate environmental load" for a given community.

EPA has begun to embrace the concept of "**community-based environmental protection**." This is an outgrowth of an appreciation that the elements of an ecosystem are more than natural and physical, but also social and cultural. It has its roots in placed-based community-wide targeted geographic initiatives and the concept of ecosystem management.[16] As we look to a new generation of environmental protection, the use of community mapping becomes a strategy to coherently integrate diverse issues, locations, and communities into a community-based planning model. The import of these tools for addressing urban revitalization/Brownfields issues is strikingly apparent.

VII.   Executive Order 12898 and Government Reinvention

Recognizing that environmental justice and the issues related to Brownfields are by their very nature cross-cutting and multi-disciplinary, the Subcommittee sought to engage a debate over the use of Executive Order 12898-- *Federal Actions to Ensure Environmental Justice in Minority and Low Income Communities*. The concept of an executive order about environmental justice was included in a Transition Paper to the Clinton-Gore Administration developed by a coalition of grassroots environmental justice groups, civil rights organizations, and scholars. Part of the vision that guided this proposal was the overriding need to reinvent the federal government and adopt a comprehensive approach toward addressing a set of related social, economic, and environmental issues, such as unequal protection, environmental racism, and disproportionate impact of environmental pollution on communities of color and low income communities.[17]

Signed by President Clinton on February 11, 1994, Executive Order 12898 called upon 17 federal agencies to develop strategic plans to address environmental justice. The agencies included EPA, the U.S. Department of Health and Human Services (HHS), the Department of Defense (DoD), the U.S. Department of Justice (DOJ), the U.S. Department of Energy (DOE), the U.S. Department of Housing and Urban Development (HUD), the U.S. Department of Transportation (DOT), the U.S. Department of Interior (DOI), and the U.S. Department of Commerce. The Executive Order also established the IWG.

The Subcommittee took the position that only such an approach can begin to address the interrelated issues associated with urban revitalization and Brownfields. Throughout the Public Dialogues, the Subcommittee posed the question of whether or not Executive Order 12898 and the IWG can be vehicles for coalescing a strategy for linking environmental justice to addressing one of the most intractable problems of our times--the state of the urban environment.

There is no greater challenge than recasting a vision of how government should work. This must start with the original and most enduring proponents of government reinvention, such as community residents engaged in overcoming systemic impediments to locally-based solutions. Environmental justice activists and many communities have taken leadership in applying their grassroots visions of healthy and sustainable communities to issues of government reinvention. In addition to the Public Dialogues, there have been many occasions--both formal and informal--where extremely worthwhile grassroots discussions of sustainability have taken place. National policy makers would benefit greatly from such discussions.

The role of the public sector is one of the most pressing issues in present American political discourse. The question reveals itself in virtually all issues surrounding the Brownfields debate, including the future of cities, urban sprawl, economic and environmental sustainability, racial polarization and social equity, defense conversion, transportation, public health, housing and residential patterns, energy conservation, materials reuse, pollution prevention, urban agriculture, job creation and career development, education, and the link between living in degraded physical environments, alienation, and destructive violence.

These issues translate into specific questions regarding (1) how the Brownfields Initiative can be most effectively implemented, and (2) a larger effort capable of coalescing the work of all federal agencies and imbuing them with a common mission capable of providing a truly authentic sign of hope to the American people.

Efforts to make Brownfields projects more effective include:

- •• linking with federal facilities cleanup and defense conversion
- •• coordinating job training and career development resources
- •• linking with transportation development, particularly inner city mass transit
- •• coordinating community wide environmental protection and public health strategies
- •• integrating pollution prevention and environmental cleanup activities
- •• linking with urban agriculture and public lands development
- •• integrating future materials use strategies and recycling
- •• incorporating energy conservation and green business development
- •• addressing housing development and residential pattern
- •• coordinating support for small business development

To approach these questions without a clear perspective on the relationship between communities and government reinvention would be imprudent. The original and most enduring proponents of government reinvention are community residents engaged in overcoming systemic impediments to locally-based solutions. The Public Dialogues illustrated in profound ways how communities have compelling visions of what constitutes healthy and sustainable communities. The heart and soul of an authentic government reinvention process is the many vibrant and coherent community-based visions of healthy and sustainable communities. Resources must be devoted to help craft these visions into coherent and compelling paradigms for positive change. Such community-based visions provide the compass for public policy discourse and government restructuring. ***By definition, genuine government reinvention cannot take place unless it is a community-driven process***.

VIII. Environmental Justice and the Next Generation of Environmental Protection

When the environmental justice movement posited the notion that "people must speak for themselves" about an environment defined as "the place where we live, where we work, and where we play," it established a framework for functionally bridging the key components of emerging environmental policy, including ecosystem management and community-based environmental protection, equal protection, pollution prevention, cumulative risk, partnership building, programmatic integration, and accountability to the public.[18] This fact needs to be elevated as a major tenet of emerging environmental policy. Environmental justice is predicated upon the fact that the health of the members of a community, both individually and collectively, is a product of physical, social, cultural, and spiritual factors. It provides a key to understanding an integrative environmental policy which treats our common ecosystem as the basis for all life (human and non-human) and activity (economic and otherwise).

A systematic public discourse over issues of race and the environment began around the siting of hazardous waste and other noxious facilities. Initially, issues of race and the environment were understood only within the narrow context of the siting issue. To a large extent, those who are out of touch with communities continue to focus only on this issue. However, the issues associated with environmental justice have grown exponentially as more and more communities demand that their day-to-day issues--be they residential, occupational, or otherwise--be made part of the discourse over environmental policy.

Moreover, there exists the need to examine ways of integrating place-based approaches to environmental protection with sector-based approaches. This has enormous implications for industrial policy. In fact, the Brownfields issue is a critical nexus for understanding the need for such integration. More likely than not, any industrial sector which has entered its second generation and beyond will have large numbers of Brownfields sites. They are the inescapable byproducts of current patterns of industrial/urban development. Far thinking economic and environmental analysts realize that one must take into account the benefits and costs of the entire "life-cycle" of an individual plant or facility or industrial sector. Failure to do so inevitably results in passing costs from one generation to another. Thus, Brownfields represent the costs which were externalized during the 1950s and must be paid for today. The urban sprawl/Brownfields issues makes it evident that the natural and human ecosystems may be fast approaching the limits of their capacity to maintain such development patterns. There are grave perils to a failure in not turning this way of doing business on its head so that such considerations are addressed at the front end.

Likewise, pollution prevention must be integrated into all Brownfields projects as an overarching principle. Brownfields projects can provide unique opportunities to apply the pollution prevention concept in practical ways. Most Brownfields communities have both cleanup and toxic release problems. Turning them into livable communities means that both have to be addressed. For example, if you do cleanup without pollution prevention, the same set of problems will reemerge. The community must be involved in developing pollution prevention strategies because they often have the most practical and innovative ideas.

Pollution prevention must be integrated into all Brownfields projects as an overarching principle. Brownfields projects can provide unique opportunities to apply the pollution prevention concept in practical ways. Most Brownfields communities have both cleanup and toxic release problems. Turning them into livable communities means that both have to be addressed. For example, if you do cleanup without pollution prevention, the same set of problems will reemerge. To date, the concept of pollution prevention has been noticeably absent from the Brownfields dialogue. To avoid yet another generation of Brownfields, pollution prevention must be aggressively introduced **before** plans for redevelopment have become entrenched. Education about pollution prevention must take place at the earliest stages. While most stakeholders have a basic understanding of pollution prevention as a general concept, residents, developers, financiers, and other stakeholders must translate this general concept into a common jargon and practical models. The community must be involved in developing pollution prevention strategies because they often have the most practical and innovative ideas. They have the most at stake when it comes to ensuring that a site never returns to its past brownfields state.

Environmental justice represents a new vision borne out of a community-driven process whose essential core is a transformative public discourse over what are truly healthy, sustainable, and vital communities. It flows out of 500 years of struggle for survival by people of color in a multiracial and multicultural society where they were excluded from the full benefits of citizenship or equal rights by one group. It was not coincidental that civil rights leader Martin Luther King, Jr. traveled to Memphis, Tennessee in 1968 to address "an economic and environmental justice dispute for sanitation workers striking for better wages, improved working conditions, and equity with other municipal workers."[19]

Over the past decade, environmental justice has made tremendous contributions to understanding the profound value of public participation and accountability in formulating public policy and making decisions about the environment. It has reshaped the discourse around public health and environment risks to include the path-breaking issue of multiple, cumulative, and synergistic risk. It has pressed for a new paradigm for conducting community-driven science and holistic place-based, and systems-wide environmental protection. Environmental justice will be the seed-bed for the development of a set of new frameworks and tools truly capable of producing physically and psychologically healthy, economically and ecologically sustainable, and culturally and spiritually vital communities.

Environmental justice is uniquely equipped to provide the visions, frameworks, and tools to address one of the most critical issues of our times. The future of America's cities is a matter of great concern not only to its residents but also to the future of habitats generally, both urban and rural. The crisis in urban America is fundamentally an ecological one--in the fullest sense of the word.[20] Indeed many issues posed in the Brownfields debate will determine America's fate not only as a society, but as a civilization. A key contribution of environmental justice over the next several years will be a transformative discourse over how to achieve healthy and sustainable communities in the 21st century.

Suggested Pollution Prevention Resources
to be Provided by EPA

Different communication tools (for example, fact sheets and handbooks) could be developed to describe the following:

Community Planning
- •• How to include pollution prevention and waste minimization into the early stages of the redevelopment planning process.
- •• Questions to ask during the planning process.
- •• Lists of federal and state contacts.

Development and Investment Tools
- •• Information on financing and insurance products to support pollution prevention and waste minimization.
- •• State and local government program options that encourage pollution prevention and waste minimization.

Technical Information
- •• Industry-specific (for example, dry cleaners, electroplaters, etc.) Products on the technical how-tos of incorporating pollution prevention and waste minimization into their facility.
- •• Information on substituting toxic substances with safer substances.
- •• Case studies of actual businesses that have adopted pollution prevention and waste minimization into their industrial or commercial processes.

URBAN REVITALIZATION/BROWNFIELDS RECOMMENDATIONS

Abandoned commercial and industrial properties called "Brownfields" which dot the urban landscape are overwhelmingly concentrated in people of color, low-income, indigenous peoples, and otherwise marginalized communities. By their very nature, Brownfields are inseparable from issues of social inequity, racial discrimination and urban decay--specifically manifested in adverse land use decisions, housing discrimination, residential segregation, community disinvestment, infrastructure decay, lack of educational and employment opportunity, and other issues.

The existence of degraded and hazardous physical environments in people of color, low-income, indigenous peoples, and otherwise disenfranchised communities, is apparent and indisputable. The physical elements of such environments, in part or in whole, have contributed to human disease and illness, negative psycho-social impact, economic disincentive, infrastructure decay, and overall community disintegration. Brownfields are merely one aspect of this phenomenon.

Environmental justice and Brownfields are inextricably linked; the inescapable context for examination of the Brownfields issue is environmental justice and urban revitalization. At the core of an environmental justice perspective is the recognition of the interconnectedness of the physical environment to the overall economic, social, human, and cultural/spiritual health of a community. The vision of environmental justice is the development of a paradigm to achieve socially equitable, environmentally healthy, economically secure, psychologically vital, spiritually whole, and ecologically sustainable communities. To this end, Brownfields redevelopment must be linked to help address this broader set of community needs and goals without creating new problems, such as displacement caused from selective revitalization. Brownfields initiatives and community planning should ensure the long-term survivability of existing communities.

Such an approach has important ramifications for the development of strategies, partnerships, models, and pilot projects. It requires a firm commitment toward achieving the goals of environmental justice and must involve the community as an equal partner. In addition, the approach must integrate activities of all federal agencies as well as their state, local, and tribal counterparts. Through these Public Dialogues, communities have articulated a highly compelling vision of the future that speaks to all levels of government. The recommendations that follow were developed within the framework of a number of overarching questions that emerged as the Subcommittee traveled across the nation and heard testimony from the participants in the Public Dialogues.

Recommendations have been grouped into three basic categories:

I.   Public Participation and Community Vision

      1.   Informed and Empowered Community Involvement
      2.   Community Vision/Comprehensive Community Based Planning
      3.   Role and Participation of Youth

II.   Key Issue Areas

      4.   Equal Protection
      5.   Public Health, Environmental Standards, and Liability
      6.   Job Creation, Training, and Career Development
      7.   Land Use

III. Public and Private Sector Partnerships

      8.   Community/Private Sector Partnerships
      9.   Local, State, Tribal, and Territorial Government
      10.   Federal Interagency Cooperation, Programmatic Integration, and Government Reinvention

Given the cross-cutting nature of the issues surrounding urban revitalization and Brownfields, these recommendations should be viewed as an integrative set. Each recommendation is an important and indispensable piece of the larger puzzle. Therefore, no single recommendation, nor a subset of recommendations, should be viewed in isolation from the others.

I. PUBLIC PARTICIPATION AND COMMUNITY VISION

1. Informed and Empowered Community Involvement

Early, ongoing, and meaningful public participation is a hallmark of sound public policy and decision making. This requires that those most directly impacted are capable of exercising effectively their prerogatives and obligations to provide public input. Hence, the Subcommittee believes that public participation is meaningless if it is not informed and empowered community involvement.

Issues typically worthy of government attention such as Brownfields are highly complex and pose real challenges to policy makers as to how to develop and master the tools, methodologies, frameworks, processes, and protocols necessary for effective and meaningful public participation. Such issues typically involve multiple communities, different cultures and languages, diverse stakeholders, time frames, multiple locations, a broad range of agencies and institutions, and other factors. More often than not, the issues involve conflicting interests, agendas, and value systems. Typically these issues involve four elements: (1) facts are uncertain, (2) values are in dispute, (3) stakes are high, and (4) a decision is urgent. While an appropriate description of the many environmentally related issues facing society today, the environmental justice framework eloquently speaks to the need for meaningful public participation in the conduct of science and use of technology.

> *"If there is any hope of revitalizing our urban communities, we have to begin with revitalizing the participation of the citizenry. We know that apathy is rampant, especially in economically disadvantaged communities. But for us to build sustainable communities, we must take the time to cut through the apathy. It will take time because people of color and low income communities are not just disenfranchised economically; we are disenfranchised psychologically because we have witnessed a history of being locked out of the decision-making process.*
>
> Connie Tucker
> Southern Organizing Committee for
> Social and Economic Justice
> Atlanta, GA, Public Dialogue

> *"I was struck by the vivid separation of the revitalization theme from the more common basis for cleanup and reuse for purposes of redevelopment. I found this to be an incisive and important distinction to make, as it provides the logical justification for the report's emphasis on community participation throughout the revitalization process. If the purpose is only redevelopment, then it can be handled as business as usual, and there is little need for public participation besides that required by law (for example, zoning or permit decisions). It is very important to be upfront and direct with this distinction."*
>
> Tom Kennedy
> Association of State and Territorial
> Solid Waste Management Officials

One key element of ensuring informed and empowered community involvement is that this participation must be early and meaningful--taking place "up front"--not an after-thought. Participants at the Public Dialogues stressed a new power relationship within which communities are an integral part of the decision-making process "from beginning to end." Unfortunately, too often communities are consulted only after a decision has been made. Too often, government response to community questions results in their operating in a "decide, adapt, and defend" mode. The community is inherently qualified to be "at the table" during discussions about matters which affect them. Moreover, several participants cautioned that just because a person was at the table does not necessarily mean they are part of the decision-making process. For example, grant proposals often create the impression that community groups are more involved in the development of a project proposal than is actually the case. This becomes a source of friction and distrust.

Government officials should be accountable for not only providing opportunities for public input, but in making a good faith effort to succeed in securing public input, it is not enough to simply hold a meeting or provide opportunities for accesss. It should be noted that Native American tribes are governmental entities--as such, the tribal members of tribal governments should be included in all public participation and outreach activities.

Meaningful participation is different in many ways from holding public meetings or getting letters of support. Participants noted that:

- • Ongoing stakeholder involvement is the only way to ensure that the affected community can influence technical and economic decisions.

- • The community brings a wealth of site-specific knowledge to the table. Ongoing mechanisms such as advisory boards allow participants to get beyond posturing and to work together cooperatively.

- • Upfront community involvement reduces the likelihood that political or legal action will block projects down the road.

It is not enough to provide access to information or opportunities to provide comment. Decision-makers must make an effort to truly consider the advice offered by the community. It is important that these decision-makers not only provide opportunities for affected communities to provide advice, but demonstrate that they are "hearing" the advice offered. Admittedly, decisions that may be selected may not agree with the recommendations offered; however, the best way to build credibility with the affected community is to show that it is seriously considering its advice.

With respect to public participation and the EPA Brownfields Initiative, there is typically much confusion around the fact that EPA's grants must go to a state, local, or tribal government. Community groups with an interest in a local Brownfields site thus may waste much time and energy because they are unaware that they need to develop strategies and build partnerships to ensure public accountability on the part of local officials and enhance the local Brownfields proposals. Most important, many community residents have both the desire to assist the city and much knowledge to offer, but lack resources and information to participate fully.

SPECIFIC RECOMMENDATIONS:

1-1. *Support sustained and structured public dialogue on Brownfields and environmental justice on all levels*.

The Subcommittee appreciates EPA's realization of the need for and its commitment to a systematic and sustained national dialogue on Brownfields and environmental justice. Such a commitment requires some structured mechanisms (such as community advisory boards) for communities to engage EPA, government and other stakeholders, around their concerns. In this case, NEJAC developed its Public Participation Model upon which the Public Dialogues were modeled. Other mechanisms--on national, regional, and local levels--must be created and supported. In addition to traditional areas of public participation (such as planning and the oversight of cleanup) the public should play a role in the review of research projects, and the development of grant proposals.

1-2. *Develop efforts to empower stakeholders through information and education. Conduct the Brownfields program in ways which offer a real sense of hope.*

Public Dialogue participants indicated that many residents of impacted communities do not participate due to despair, apathy, lack of time and resources, or because they have just given up. In addition to specific recommendations to ensure better access, ranging from holding meetings at convenient times and accessible places to use of non-traditional outreach methods, the Subcommittee also emphasizes the need for government to foster encouragement and a sense of hope that is based upon results. In addition to participation in the decision-making process, residents must also participate in any social, environmental, and economic benefits that results from decisions. The education process also must include ways to provide communities with enough tools and information so they understand they can influence the political process beyond existing mechanisms.

1-3. ***Undertake special outreach efforts to overlooked groups.***

Even programs that are targeted to communities of color still overlook key sectors of impacted communities. Examples cited during the Public Dialogues include Laotian Americans in Richmond, California; Arab-Americans in Detroit, Michigan; and Native Americans in various urban areas. At the same time, each of these groups has unique historical and cultural circumstances which must be considered.

---

1. ACTION ITEMS

- • 1a. Institute policies and performance measures which encourage program personnel and policy makers to spend substantive time in neighborhoods as a regular part of their work so that there is understanding of real problems, concerns, and aspirations of community residents.

- • 1b. Define "community" at each site in a way that is inclusive but gives priority to people who live or work closest to a site and/or are most directly impacted by activities at the site.

- • 1c. Implement mechanisms and structures through which the community can take part in reviewing and evaluating progress.

- • 1d. Institute ways to improve the public's access to information on urban revitalization/Brownfields, including:

- • Support the establishment of "storefront" type clearinghouses and repositories of Brownfields information in impacted communities for open access to information and create atmosphere for ongoing dialogue and planning (a good example is the Brownfields pilot project in Northhampton County/Cape Charles, Virginia)

- • Hold meetings at convenient times and locations

- • Provide day care and translation

- • Utilize innovative and non-traditional outreach methods such as school programs, posters, advertisements in local papers, community newsletters, and electronic mail

- • Build upon existing social and cultural networks such as schools, churches, and civic organizations

- • 1e. Institute procedures and protocols to verify demonstrable partnerships with community-based groups in project proposals. Prospective grants and other support to city, state, and tribal governments should contain specific agreed language regarding, and be adequately funded to support, continuing public participation, such as the establishment of community advisory boards made up of people most impacted by Brownfields sites.

- • 1f. Conduct an inventory of the language resources available for serving potentially-impacted communities.

- • 1g. Convene a summit meeting of all stakeholders working on or affected by Brownfields projects as an opportunity to bring together all parties to discuss critical issues, craft unified strategies, and determine actions for follow-up.

2.   ***Community Vision/Comprehensive Community-Based Planning***

There exists within local communities highly coherent, vibrant, and compelling visions for achieving healthy and sustainable communities. Such visions, particularly in people of color, low income, indigenous peoples, and otherwise marginalized communities, emerge from a long history of grassroots efforts to be self-defined, self-directed, self-empowered, self-controlled, self-sufficient, and self-determined. Many communities already are engaging in highly successful planning and visioning processes. Government must acknowledge that these already exist. Brownfields and all community revitalization efforts must be based upon such community visions. The capacity of local communities to identify and build upon the assets which ensure that a healthy and sustainable community, is an invaluable resource to the nation. These assets are economic, social, human, institutional, physical, natural, cultural, intellectual, and spiritual in nature.

Public Dialogue participants articulated the importance of developing holistic, multi-faceted, interactive, and integrative community-based planning models for Brownfields and urban revitalization. They view community-based planning as an alternative to the current dependence on developer-driven models that traditionally define the Brownfields problem in a narrow way. Community-based planning is a framework for identifying and solving problems. Instead of addressing problems piecemeal and then applying a "one-size fits all" solution, community-based planning has the flexibility to confront problems in the context of the region, the ecosystem, the city, or the neighborhood in which they occur.

> *"Periodically, societies need to create movements that stretch our humanity as we transform ourselves and our environment at the same time. It's been very exciting to be a part of such a movement. I will try to convey in a few words what is happening so that you can catch the spirit...I'm convinced that out of the devastation of Detroit, we are at the point here today where we can really redefine, rebuild, respirit, and recivilize the city. As you drive through Detroit, it's very easy to see the vacant lots and the abandoned buildings. What is harder to see behind the physical devastation is the new spirit that is arising in the city and finds its expression chiefly in the explosion of meetings that has taken place in the last year. There are meetings of hundreds and thousands of people, namely around the empowerment zone and the Land Use Task Force...But there are smaller meetings. For example, there's a group called Healthy Detroit, of which the Mayor is the honorary chair... Here in Detroit, we started by building a common vision."*
>
> Grace Boggs
> Detroiters for Environmental Justice
> Detroit, MI, Public Dialogue

> *"What would Detroit be like if there was a call to put major resources into economic self-reliance that would create economic livelihood opportunities in communities? A vision is what has been portrayed but has never been. It raises one's sights of what might be. It's inspiring and hopeful.... What would a new community-based economy look like? It must be real and tangible and immediate. I can see it, I can touch it, I can almost taste it...*
>
> *"If we ignore the development of an urban agricultural base in Detroit, we will miss the opportunity to really make Detroit a great city. In the 21st century, only those cities that develop a sound policy of such urban, social, and ecological developments will flourish. I believe that we will only move forward toward this future if we begin to adopt and integrate the Principles of Environmental Justice into our day-to-day fabric, and that's the future that I look forward to."*
>
> John Gruchala
> Wayne County Community College
> Detroit, MI, Public Dialogue

In the eyes of the community, the Brownfields issue is more than the simple identification of contaminated sites and goes beyond the definitions created by developers. The community defines the problem from the vantage point of their aspirations. There was support for this premise from virtually all Public Dialogue participants, including representatives of the business community and lending institutions. Each realized that "if we're not addressing transportation, housing, education and training, and racism and other driving factors that have led to deindustrialization of our urban areas and loss of vitality, then addressing Brownfields, environmental contamination and liability alone will not be a significant benefit for people in the communities."

SPECIFIC RECOMMENDATIONS:

2-1. **Base Brownfields pilots and other efforts upon coherent community visions which emerge from processes that have _integrity_ within a community by ensuring opportunities for communities to articulate their own visions for "redefining, rebuilding, and respiriting" their communities.**

Such visions must be comprehensive and address community revitalization, education, environmental cleanup and redevelopment, job creation and training, economic impacts, housing, and development of institutional infrastructures. Several participants at the Public Dialogues pointed to local efforts to build common visions that allow people from various backgrounds to come together and form a common vision that incorporates the needs of different sectors of the population.

2-2. **Acknowledge community-based planning as a critical methodology for environmental protection and promote its use both inside and outside the Agency.**

Several participants spoke about the need to develop tools that can be placed in the hands of community members which can help them to address issues related to environmental justice, community-based planning, and urban revitalization. They noted the importance of using such tools when forming a collective community vision. Participants pointed to numerous examples of community-based planning tools, including:

•• South Bronx/NYC Ordinance 197A Planning Process (Vernice Miller-Northeast Environmental Justice Network)
•• Southwest Detroit Environmental Vision Project (Ed Miller-Charles Stewart Mott Foundation)
•• San Diego Toxic Free Neighborhoods Community Planning
•• Guide (Diane Takvorian-Environmental Health Coalition)
•• Pocket of Poverty Neighborhood Alliance Strategic Plan (Teresa Cordova-University of New Mexico at Albuquerque).

2-3. **Support community-based efforts to link Brownfields projects to other redevelopment and community enhancement strategies such as "Empowerment Zones/Enterprise Communities, workforce development and job training, transportation infrastructure development, federal facility cleanup, and others.**

Virtually every federal agency has at least one program that addresses urban revitalization. However, these programs are not coordinated and appear, to impacted communities, to be at cross-purposes. This link should be done both at the federal policy level and in the field.

2-4. **Encourage revitalization strategies and redevelopment efforts which serve to support, enhance and protect a community's culture and history.**

Such efforts should take into account both local and regional history. They should seek opportunities to build upon cultural resources and efforts at historical preservation as vehicles for economic development and enhancement of community-based assets.

2. ACTION ITEMS

• • 2a. Compile an inventory of the resources available within the Agency (such as LAND VIEW II and other mapping programs) and outside of the Agency (such as an inventory of relevant extramural literature, experiences, experts, tools, and practicing institutions) as part of its community-based environmental protection efforts.

• • 2b. Develop programs to provide to the community access to and training on the use of LAND VIEW II, geographic information systems (GIS) and other electronic mapping resources.

• • 2c. Develop pilot programs for place-based coordination of Federal agency activities.

• • 2d. Provide training opportunities to communities in the use of community-based planning techniques.

• • 2e. Develop guidance for incorporation of community-based planning and community visioning into Community-Based Environmental Protection initiatives.

• • 2f. Convene a national roundtable on strategies for application and development of GIS and community mapping tools.

3. *Role and Participation of Youth*

Young people provided great energy, creativity, and a sense of fresh vision to the Public Dialogues. During the meetings, they insisted on participating in all dialogues and decision-making processes. They made some of the most compelling presentations. For example, the Public Dialogues yielded perhaps no more thought provoking testimony than the account of a 5-year old African American boy's unsolicited remark in which he associated being black with living in burnt-out, empty, trash-filled neighborhoods.

Environmental justice seeks to address the functional link between living in degraded physical environments, mass alienation, and destructive violence. Offering a coherent way to impact this relationship will significantly benefit greatly those seeking to address violence, substance abuse, and related issues.

Many issues associated with Brownfields are profoundly related to the concerns of youth. The issues of healthy and sustainable communities are issues of a viable future. Government and social institutions have a moral obligation to ensure a world fit for all children--present and future. The youth are a precious resource which must be affirmed, supported, and nurtured.

> *"We have to talk about a vision that comes from the community, but part of that community is young people. It can't just be in words alone. It really has to be about involving the young people into the process...*
>
> *"One of the young people who works with us, a brother, often says that the solutions of today end up being the problems of tomorrow. If young people are not sitting in on the process, are not involved in the dialogue--I can understand how the solutions for today will end up being the problems of tomorrow...*
>
> *"[Young people] must be part of revitalizing our urban inner cities. In so doing, we must look at building partnerships with elementary schools, high schools. I know here in Atlanta there are many schools which are built on top of landfills. Whether or not they are cleaned up, the history is there. How many of our children know that? How many of our parents actually know that? We must look at the psychological impact on young people today.*
>
> *"When you look at the reality of lack of jobs, when you look at the question of jobs versus the environment, we hear that, as young people, we don't understand the dialogue that is taking place around being able to develop real jobs that affect our future so that our community can be truly sustainable.*
>
> *"When you look at crime and violence in the communities, it is all linked. Yet what it comes down to is the reality of how to overcome these things. The psychological impact on young people growing up in urban American must be filtered into our public dialogue as we talk about revitalization."*
>
> **Angela Brown**
> **Youth Task Force**
> **Atlanta, GA, Public Dialogue**

Any discussion of Brownfields revitalization, to be successful, must involve the participation of the youth in urban areas where Brownfields dominate. These youths will eventually be the decision makers for their communities in the future. Therefore, to avoid making today's solutions tomorrow's dilemma for the youth, it is essential to get their input.

The youths living in Brownfields areas often are already familiar with these sites. While they may be unfamiliar with the term "Brownfields," they are aware of the opportunities presented by these sites. For example, in some inner-city neighborhoods youths utilize some of these sites to engage in urban wildlife preservation. They also can be found in many cities using Brownfields areas as sites where they raise pigeons as a hobby. The youths take on the responsibility for providing the nurturing environment these birds need to thrive. Such activities are akin to those of organizations that raise endangered species in captivity. In our attempts to involve youth in discussions about Brownfields revitalization, we can take advantage of the initiative demonstrated by these youth.

Additionally, meaningful employment and career prospects rank among the central questions facing young persons--in many ways defining young people's sense of identity and connectedness to society.

These are issues which must be engaged at the earliest age possible. EPA and other government agencies must see it as their responsibility to work with young people to help present a message about meaningful career prospects that are relevant to them.

SPECIFIC RECOMMENDATIONS:

3-1. *Form the requisite partnerships both inside and outside of government to better understand and address urban revitalization/Brownfields issues of concern to youth.*

3-2. *Through the Brownfields initiative, integrate environmental activities and career development with targeted environmental justice and urban revitalization strategies.*

A significant amount of resources and attention is devoted to engage young persons in the pursuit of careers related to the environmental. Environmental justice and urban revitalization create opportunities to make current educational programs more relevant by integrating study and action around issues related to "the place where we live, work, and play." Public education can be engaged in highly productive and compelling ways. EPA should partner with other agencies to support efforts by public schools, community colleges, public and private universities, and other educational institutions to integrate these issues.

Environmental justice and urban revitalization also offer opportunities to change the serious inadequacy of cultural diversity in EPA and professions related to the environment. Moreover, they allow for integration across disciplinary lines to make for career paths more relevant to the needs of the 21st century.

3-3. *Expand environmental education opportunities for urban youth through urban environmental education centers.*

Revitalization of Brownfields sites also present the opportunity to expand the education for inner-city youth. These sites could be converted to urban environmental education centers that could serve as a mechanism through which youth could engage in environmental educational activities. Since Brownfields sites are the result of past environmental practices, these centers could focus on activities that promote the long-term sustainability of cities, and in turn, of the sites themselves. Experiential education programs take youth from urban areas to camps outside the city to train them on team building activities. The environmental education centers could assume the function of these experiential programs directly in the neighborhoods in which the youth live. Such a change also allows for a curriculum that focuses on issues (such as environmental justice) that these youths face on a daily basis. These centers also increase the possibility that any solutions adopted for Brownfields revitalization today will be long-term or permanent. By incorporating youth ideas and initiatives now, we reduce the possibility that these youths, when they become adults will fundamentally alter initiatives and solutions we adopt now.

YouthBuild

The YouthBuild program is an innovative and successful program that responds to two problems that pervade low-income communities: the need to reach out to at-risk youth and the shortage of safe, affordable housing. YouthBuild teaches low-income youth how to provide housing for their communities by engaging them in four mutually supportive areas:

•• education
•• employment training
•• leadership development
•• housing construction and rehabilitation

In the classroom, students receive both academic education and skills instruction. On the construction sites, with appropriate supervision, the students rehabilitate abandoned buildings in poor communities-- creating affordable housing while gaining construction skills.

YouthBuild has received national recognition for its effectiveness in providing disadvantaged youth with direction and hope, while simultaneously addressing the need for affordable housing in low-income communities.

3-4. ***Provide support for youth-led projects.***

One proposed method to involve youth is through the YouthBuild program. Because YouthBuild is a national organization with sites in most major cities, it provides an opportunity to solicit ideas from, and the involvement of a core group of youth nationwide. Another noteworthy example is *Commencement 2000*, an environmental education urban forestry project in Oakland, California initiated by the U.S. Forest Service.

3-5. ***Establish mechanisms which enhance multi-generational partnerships, particularly supporting the establishment and maintenance of youth mentoring networks--both formal and informal.***

---

3. ACTION ITEMS

- • 3a. Designate "youth" as a formal stakeholder category for federal advisory committees and other multi-stakeholder public participation processes.

- • 3b. Support efforts to develop youth mapping and planning projects, such as Kids City in Cleveland Ohio.

- • 3c. Conduct a conference on youth concerns and needs around urban revitalization/Brownfields.

- • 3d. Work with the U.S. Department of Education to develop educational programs around urban revitalization and Brownfields which can be used in public schools.

- • 3e. Review current environmental education programs to ensure that they address environmental justice, urban revitalization, and job training, and career development concerns.

II. *KEY ISSUE AREAS*

4. *Equal Protection*

The Brownfields problem--the profusion of abandoned and/or contaminated properties in people of color, low income, indigenous peoples, and marginalized communities--cannot be separated from unequal protection in housing, land use, transportation, educational and economic opportunity, and other issues related to urban deterioration.

The Brownfields issue focuses attention on yet another important set of equal protection issues, i.e.,

> "To the extent practical and permitted by law, and consistent with the principles set forth in the report on the National Performance Review, each Federal agency shall make achieving environmental justice part of its mission by identifying and addressing , as appropriate, disproportionately high and adverse human health or environmental effects of its programs, policies, and activities on minority populations and low-income populations in the United States and its territories and possessions, the District of Columbia, the Commonwealth of Puerto Rico, and the Commonwealth of the Mariana Islands. "
>
> Executive Order 12898
> February 11, 1994

urban sprawl. Historical land use patterns placed people of color and the poor in undesirable residential areas near industrial activity. These areas suffer a double burden as current transportation policies promote disinvestment and place substantial indirect burdens on such communities and local economies. Many federal investments, particularly in areas of transportation, have helped to widen divisions in society by increasing the physical gaps that separate poor and from socioeconomic opportunities in the increasingly distant periphery, and by economically isolating central business districts.

In certain urban areas, urban sprawl is infringing upon nearby Tribal lands and, as such, is creating direct burdens on environmental, social, economic, and cultural values. In other urban areas, Tribal governments have won land claim settlements that provide for Tribal acquisition of urban lands that have included contaminated and potentially contaminated commercial and industrial areas. It is imperative that local jurisdictions that are located next to Tribal land pay attention to the concerns of the Tribal governments, as well as its Tribal community members. Urban revitalization and Brownfields programs must recognize ceded lands, fee lands, and all lands possessing historical, cultural, and spiritual values.

Equal protection is the constitutional right of all Americans. This demands that equal opportunity be made accessible to all people, regardless of social or economic standing. Environmental justice needs to be distinguished from a narrow view of equal protection that stops at merely making exposure from harmful pollutants more evenly distributed. "What is ultimately at stake in the environmental justice debate is everyone's quality of life. The goal is equal protection, not equal pollution."[21]

SPECIFIC RECOMMENDATIONS:

4-1. *Make use of Executive Order 12898 to bring about coordinated implementation by multiple federal agencies of programs related to urban revitalization and Brownfields.*

4-2. *Intensify efforts for ensuring cultural diversity within the workforce of all federal agencies, viewing this as a key foundational element to the success of initiatives such as urban revitalization/Brownfields.*

4-3. *Examine use of Title VI of the Civil Rights Act of 1964 with respect to federal support in areas of community reinvestment, fair housing, equal business opportunity, financing, and health protection.*

---

4. ACTION ITEMS

• • 4a. Intensify efforts for ensuring cultural diversity within the EPA workforce, viewing this as a key foundational element to initiatives such as Brownfields.

• • 4b. Develop analytical models of the distributional impacts of federal programs on urban sprawl and incorporate such analyses in the National Environmental Policy Act environmental justice guidance.

• • 4c. Identify all Tribal lands that are impacted by urban sprawl and evaluate barriers against equal protection.

---

5. *Public Health, Environmental Standards, and Liability*

Public health and environmental protection are matters of primary concern to communities; they were a recurring theme of testimony presented at the Public Dialogues. Public Dialogue participants pointed out that thousands of abandoned and contaminated sites are located in densely populated urban areas close to where children, teenagers, and homeless people play and congregate. These also are areas for large-scale commercial and illegal dumping of contaminated materials. Any economic redevelopment strategy must be cognizant of pressing public health issues in communities; it must not sacrifice environmental safety for the sake of economic growth or prosperity.

Many Public Dialogue participants expressed uneasiness about the environmental and public health ramifications of present approaches to Brownfields redevelopment. The Subcommittee believes that there are enormous social costs attached to our inability to return appropriate properties to beneficial reuse. In addition to the loss of economic vitality in terms of employment, commerce, and taxes, abandoned properties become a magnet for criminal and drug activity, a source of community demoralization, and a contributor to a downward spiral of community decay.

The Subcommittee has ascertained that while the prospect of quickly returning abandoned properties to beneficial reuse may be highly attractive, communities are extremely apprehensive that attempts to streamline or speed up the cleanup process may be at the expense of environmental protection and public health. These are extremely complex issues where decisions which may determine the fate of communities for generations to come. The Subcommittee believes that any

"One of the first times I heard the notion of Brownfields was from the environmental attorney for one of the nation's largest corporations. She told me that she liked the idea of Brownfields because that meant that they could build factories in communities that were already contaminated rather than going out and threatening the Greenfields, which were pristine. Having sat in hearings for the Defense Department and Energy Department where they talked about relaxing cleanup standards based on prospective reuse of the property, I think there are a lot of people in government who have basically the same attitude. We pollute certain areas of the country; there are certain kinds of people that live there. Let's keep on polluting the same areas. If Brownfields get misused as a concept, it could lead to more of that.

"What we heard today, however, is that people in most communities don't see it that way. They don't figure that just because they were polluted by an oil company, a utility, or a roadway, that somehow their families should be subjected to more. So the message we have heard--and it has to go back to Washington loud and clear--is that you look at a way of first cleaning up the property, and secondly, developing industry, economic activity, or parks."

Lenny Siegel
Pacific Studies Center
Oakland, CA, Public Dialogue

"Revitalizing abandoned or underused industrial or commercial land under a Brownfields Initiative must be based on total community planning to change existing conditions of social inequity, racial discrimination, and urban decay. The poor have found it economically necessary to live in undesirable residential areas. Historically, this included poor immigrants from Europe early in this century, poor whites who lived on "the other side of the tracks" in both urban and rural areas, and the majority of people of color. Prior to automobiles and public transportation, laborers lived within walking distance of factories where they worked.

"Building a new factory in a poorly-planned and zoned urban site will not correct basic urban problems. Sound environmental health planning and zoning is the only solution. Most industrial areas were developed before cities started to address planning and zoning concerns, and were concentrated around harbors, rivers, and rail lines. Economic pressures still override environmental justice for the poor. Where industrial uses (including highway systems, incinerators, and sewage treatment plants) are located in residential neighborhoods, steps should be taken to either relocated through land swaps, the offending industry or the residences.

Dr. Andrew McBride
City of Stamford, CT, Department of Health

"rush to judgement" or the adoption of a "one size fits all" solution to Brownfields assessment, cleanup, and redevelopment, would be imprudent. More important, the Subcommittee has ascertained that there is as yet an insufficient level of discussion about these complex issues in directly impacted communities. Ultimately, these communities must be part of the process of shaping these policies and practical solutions. Thus, the Subcommittee is not prepared to endorse particular solutions until directly impacted communities have had a chance to provide visible and meaningful input to this discussion.

The Subcommittee's viewpoints on Public Health, Environmental Standards, and Liability issues can be summarized in the following way:

Public Health: In most urban/Brownfields areas, there exists a set of characteristics which contribute to overall poor health. For this reason, a new set of priorities is needed. For good reasons, methodologies and technologies for characterizing environmental hazards heretofore have been built around the "worst first model." High priority has been given by responsible parties, regulators, and communities to identity and define the contamination that posed the greatest threat to public health or the environment, given existing exposures and potential pathways.

For Brownfields, that priority is turned on its head. To maximize the reuse of large areas where there exists a multiplicity of smaller sources of contamination with greatly variable degrees of severity, the cleanup process needs to determine early on which areas are safe. Only then is it healthy and economically viable to transfer or reuse a particular property or proceed towards an overall revitalization strategy for the area. In order to ensure public health and a sound environment as part of both short term and long term integrated redevelopment plans, the goal must be to ascertain not only what sites are unsafe but what areas are safe.

The primary and most cost-effective public health strategy is prevention. In the less than perfect world of congested, post-industrial urban/Brownfields communities, the Subcommittee believes that there

---

Brownfields Initiatives and Community Planning

Brownfields initiatives and community planning should include:

- Sound and equitable planning and zoning with environmental justice review
- Community involvement with participation by poor and people of color
- Air pollution, water pollution, noise pollution
- Soil contamination (lead, petroleum, heavy metals, asbestos, etc.)
- Visual pollution (billboards, poorly maintained properties, poor architecture)
- Refuse sanitation (removal of litter, refuse, adequate storage receptacles)
- Municipal sanitary sewers, public water supply
- Public transportation, adequate streets, parking, traffic flow
- Pedestrian and handicap access
- Services (stores, schools, medical, etc)
- Quality of life facilities (parks, libraries, community centers, churches, playgrounds, programs for youths, adults and seniors)
- Landscaping (trees, mini-parks, shrubbery, flowers)
- Personal safety (police, fire, ambulance)
- Magnet facilities (parks, shopping, college, restaurants, museum, theater)
- Optimizing natural resources (waterfront, views)
- Employment for adults, youth
- Owner-occupied modest, moderate, and high-income housing

Dr. Andrew McBride
City of Stamford, CT, Department of Health

---

must be a baseline understanding of public health and environment which includes consideration of (1) characteristics of urban/Brownfields communities, (2) sources of environmental risk, (3) aggregate toxic load, and (4) the capacity of public health community to intervene effectively. The community must be engaged in developing this baseline understanding as well as making choices over redevelopment strategies. Based upon such a baseline understanding, choices can be made about revitalization and redevelopment which (1) separate people from toxics, (2) ensure environmental quality and ecological integrity, (3) create a repository of information for regulators, health practitioners, and the community, and (4) allow such choices to be based upon a rational, commonly understood, and mutually agreed upon frame of reference.

Environmental Standards: Overall community goals regarding environmental quality and land use must guide the process for developing environmental cleanup standards. This principle is crucial for the following reason. When development-oriented corporations or local governments attempt to limit cleanup time and expense by adopting weaker goals, they often end up allowing present contamination to determine the land use. Thus, they limit the community's future land use because they are unable or unwilling to carry out the cleanup.

To ensure that standards remain protective of public health, the guidelines listed below should apply to the adaptation of soil cleanup standards based upon anticipated land use. No matter which specific law is used to make these determinations, a fundamental principle applies: the decision should be made by, or in consultation with, those most directly affected or likely to be affected by the contamination.

• • The migration of hazards and the impact of contamination on adjacent areas should be considered.

• • The potential for mixed uses, such as childcare centers in industrial or commercial areas, should be evaluated.

• • The standard could take into account the potential changes of use that might take place over the life of the hazard. Relying upon current uses or even existing plans could lock in uses that the community will want to change later.

• • The cost and delay of determining and evaluating the impact of future use may make the strongest standard--such as cleanup to meet a residential scenario--the most timely and cost effective.

• • Land and water not cleaned up to the strongest standard should be subject to institutional controls and/or monitoring for the life of the hazards. The cost of these controls should be considered in evaluating the savings achieved by implementing the proposed weaker standard. The community must be involved in the decision-making process and in providing oversight and monitoring.

Even if these guidelines are followed, communities and officials should proceed cautiously. An area that has been blighted by contamination could be subjected to repeated pollution if the future use plan for that area assumes that contamination--both old and new--won't result in human illness.

The Subcommittee notes that discussions are taking place to develop a more rationale approach towards categorizing levels of severity and/or future land use in order to cut down on confusion and unnecessary bureaucracy. While the Subcommittee urges further discussions of this nature, it believes that they must be guided by the goal of achieving public health and be fully informed by the issues we have presented.

Environmental Liability: Business representatives with an interest in urban revitalization have warned that potential environmental liability is a major deterrent in Brownfields reinvestment. EPA is developing a suite of tools for overcoming liability obstacles. The Subcommittee summarizes two major points on this question:

- Community representatives generally have taken no position on these tools for addressing liability obstacles. However, they express much skepticism. They want to be sure that a responsible party is held accountable in tangible and meaningful ways. In addition, the existence of a deterrent to irresponsible and inappropriate practices is viewed as a necessity. The liability issue cannot be considered in isolation. Public Dialogue witnesses gave examples of illegal dumping and other improper and/or illegal activities in their neighborhoods. Hence, the liability issue must be considered in relationship to the existence or lack of tangible and meaningful enforcement and compliance activity, as well as mechanisms to ensure that health and related needs are met.

- The participants at the Public Dialogues point out that environmental liability is not the only impediment to reinvestment in urban/Brownfields communities. In fact, environmental liability may not rank as the most serious impediment for communities experiencing a long history of disinvestment. These other impediments include redlining and other discriminatory practices of lending and insurance institutions. They also include decisions to relocate industrial facilities to other parts of the country and the world.

Community involvement must be an overarching principle guiding Brownfields Initiatives. The community is uniquely qualified to make choices over environmental health and clean up. Community residents have direct knowledge of the environmental problems in their communities. They should be directly involved in the oversight of cleanup **and** related environmental activity and in the development of future use plans.

However, liability can be used constructively to derive positive incentives for Brownfields revitalization, rather than acting as a barrier to cleanup. But, release from liability must be used carefully to achieve these ends. The Subcommittee believes that liability should only be released once a protective cleanup has been complete, and then only with routine provisions for reopening should additional contamination be discovered or the remedy fails. In addition, there should be a clear legal understanding of responsibilities among former and prospective owners as to who has liability responsibility should the land use standards be changed sometime in the future. Other parties involved in the transaction including lenders, investors, and insurers should have clear release from liability unless they are otherwise directly responsible for the contamination, or practices causing contamination.

It is the Subcommittee's understanding that currently only designated agencies of the Federal government may release responsible parties from CERCLA liability, yet the parties most likely to be involved at potential Brownfields sites will rarely receive federal attention in the cleanup of their sites because those sites are below the levels of contamination which have prompted federal interest (such as sites proposed or listed on the NPL). To ensure that release from liability only follows successful and adequate cleanups, consideration should be given to delegating such liability release to the State agency directly overseeing the site cleanup.

The Subcommittee feels strongly that cleanup standards for Brownfields must stand on their own merits, and be based on protection needs, future land use, and the level and type of contamination present. Cleanup standards are not dependent on liability, but liability should only be released once the necessary cleanup standards are successfully achieved.

Finally, it is important to recall the advice of the community members during the Public Dialogues: liability is but one of the many inhibitions to urban revitalization--we should not put undue emphasis on the release of liability. We also need to encourage redevelopment through other incentives that will enhance property values, such as improved transportation and housing; better public services, daycare, schools; and improved public safety. All of these public choices require the active and direct participation of the community in the continuing public dialogue process which is central to this report.

SPECIFIC RECOMMENDATIONS:

5-1. *Involve the impacted community in clarifying the environmental risk issues associated with urban revitalization and Brownfields, in developing a framework for understanding and addressing the public health baseline in urban areas as part of any revitalization strategy; support right-to-know, enforcement and compliance activity in impacted communities.*

Presently, there exists a huge gap in understanding the actual environmental health challenges posed by Brownfields-type communities. For example, communities oversaturated with environmental hazards pose environmental risks to residents which is multiple, cumulative and synergistic in nature. This calls into question environmental protection models which presently proceed from a substance-specific, site-specific, and media-specific framework. In addition, EPA must provide opportunities for communities to be involved in inspections, negotiations, and public review.

5-2. *Support community desires to foster ecological restoration and incorporate sustainable development through "green" businesses, pollution prevention, and other environmentally sound economic development.*

5-3. *Support the development of, and participate in, a leadership training institute or program for minorities and the poor.*

This institute would not be a course in ecology or environmental epidemiology, but would be a course in leadership skills development for participating in important organizations, such as local planning and zoning boards, environmental community action groups, and environmental health agencies.

5-4. **Conduct training of staff personnel about public health and use as a starting point, the World Health Organization definitions of health as •a state of complete physical, mental, and social well-being, not merely the absence of disease or infirmity,• and of a healthy community as one which •includes a clean, safe, high-quality environment and a sustainable ecosystem; the provision of basic needs; an optimum level of appropriate high quality, accessible health and sick-care services; and a diverse, vital economy.•**

5. ACTION ITEMS

• • 5a. Establish mechanisms which ensure a primary role for impacted communities in the decision-making process regarding public health and environmental protection issues.

• • 5b. Support several Brownfields initiatives where the key component is assessment of health and ecological risks on a community-wide basis.

• • 5c. Support and develop strategies to address liability and insurance barriers to Brownfields redevelopment. If this requires statutory change, that change should be sought.

• • 5d. Focus attention and resources on special issues such as lack of institutional infrastructure along the US-Mexico border and on Native American reservations.

• • 5e. Support efforts to identity and clarify all issues related to reinvestment in urban/Brownfields areas, particularly the relationship between redlining, community reinvestment, and environmental liability reform.

• • 5f. Take concrete measures to address health and safety in workplaces associated with Brownfields projects.

• • 5g. Enlist appropriate federal agencies in developing a plan to ensure that public health be integrated into all urban revitalization/Brownfields initiatives as an overarching principle.

• • 5h. Conduct a series of dialogues on integration of public health and planning for purposes of achieving true urban revitalization with healthy and sustainable Brownfields redevelopment.

• • 5i. Enlist community-based organizations and national health groups such as the National Association of City and County Health Officials, American Public Health Association, American Lung Association, National Medical Association, Healthy Cities, Association of State and Territorial Health Officials, and others in ensuring that strong public health approaches towards urban revitalization/Brownfields.

6. *Job Creation, Training, and Career Development*

Brownfields redevelopment must be coordinated with broader strategies of job creation, training, and career development which produce demonstrable benefits for the host community. The startup and nurturing of locally-based businesses as a function of true economic development is a critical requirement.

Many participants stated that in order for urban areas to survive, new ways of creating and sustaining employment must be devised. They noted that if poor education, lack of training, and other issues which have led to the deindustrialization of urban areas

> *"We started in our community a Water Conservation Program with six employees. Now we have 28 employees, all [working at] $8.00 an hour and with medical insurance...We give the low-flush toilet to the community. We receive $25 for each toilet. That's the way we make [our] money. We now have this project for four years. When it started, we planned to have the program for only six months; then it continued for another six months, and another six months... We have help from the Water Department. We don't need to go through other people [to] train the kids. We have people in the organization to train these people. I think all communities can do something like this. Start low and then go up."*
>
> Juana Gutierrez
> Mothers of East Los Angeles
> Oakland, CA, Public Dialogue

continue to prevail, any effort at urban revitalization will not result in significant benefits to urban communities. These witnesses strongly urged coordination between workforce development and training programs with sustainable job opportunities. To integrate job training and employment development, urban revitalization/Brownfields initiatives should involve integrated project planning, in which the workforce needs of the various projects in an area are known soon enough to recruit and train needed workers from the local population.

Two issues were particularly prominent: (1) efforts must be made to ensure workplace health and safety for those jobs developed within the community, particularly those associated with environmental cleanup activities; and (2) jobs must produce livable wages which fit into a career development ladder that is based upon realistic assessment of present and emerging job markets.

The importance to the community of building community-based businesses and providing entrepreneurial startup help and ongoing business training to individuals and companies, with emphasis on people of color and female-owned companies within the community, was a very significant concern at the Public Dialogues.

The need to coordinate resources available for job training and business development from among the many Federal agencies with interests and funding sources was cited as a serious concern. At the present time there appears to be no "one-stop shopping" for worker training assistance, nor business development assistance. This is particularly true of the programs available from DOL, HUD, DOT, DOE, and DoD. There are many cross currents at work with the eligibility requirements that make much of the training assistance illusory to the very people within the community who need it most. The definitional problems of fitting into present "displaced" worker and similar job training programs need to be dealt with if this type of assistance is to be made meaningful to the Brownfields impacted communities.

Coordination and cooperation among government (federal, state, tribal, and local), business/industry, community-based organizations labor unions, faith groups, and the community-at-large is mandatory in order to leverage resources, avoid duplication and develop mechanisms which link workforce development and cleanup to economic redevelopment. Concentration by these parties must be on a *win/win* basis. Everyone benefits if they are unified and taking actions towards a common goal, i.e., a vibrant, safe, healthy, and sustainable community.

SPECIFIC RECOMMENDATIONS:

6-1. *Make use of the momentum generated by the Brownfields issue and provide leadership in building partnerships and coalitions which result in locally-based job creation, entrepreneurial development, and sustainable careers.*

This effort must involve all federal agencies, state, local, and tribal governments, local community development organizations, churches, labor unions, philanthropies, universities, and the business community. Specific efforts here could include encouraging new industry to hire locally and encouraging the inclusion of business and industry that is capable of long-term success and growth.

6-2. *Support efforts to ensure worker health and safety.*

Any increase in economic redevelopment activity must have a commensurate increase in support to protect worker health and safety for efforts to ensure worker health and safety, which means including support for pre-training, training and apprenticeship programs focusing on workplace safety and health. Many of these programs are now supported at local community colleges and union/management training and apprentice programs.

6-3. *Partner with other federal agencies to link clean up of federal facilities and base-conversion activities with the needs of urban revitalization and Brownfields.*

In many places, DOD and DOE facility cleanup and conversion constitute a major, if not the major, source of economic redevelopment funding potential.

6-4. *Encourage EPA and other Federal, State, local, and tribal governments to maximize the use of recycled and reused materials; local businesses should be encouraged to set similar procurement policies.*

6. ACTION ITEMS

• • 6a. Partner with other federal agencies to link rehabilitation of low- and middle-income housing stocks to EPA's Brownfields and urban revitalization projects. For example, EPA should link with HUD to address issues related to asbestos and lead abatement.

• • 6b. Continue to work with:

• • DOL to link local private industry councils with Brownfields initiatives.

• • The National Institute of Environmental Health Sciences to ensure that NIEHS Minority Worker Training pilot grants--established to facilitate the development of urban minority youth worker training programs--overlap with Brownfields pilot cities.

• • Other federal agencies (such as DOL and HUD) to develop a registered apprenticeship program called Superfund Step-Up to focus on employment opportunities for low-income and minority youth affected by contaminated waste sites.

• • 6c. Inform the community of available job- and training-related initiatives (such as Step-Up and YouthBuild) available within EPA.

• • 6d. Support efforts to provide information about technical assistance, pilot job training, and career development programs; consider a wide variety of school-to-work and youth apprenticeship programs that may be applicable to community development models involved in the Brownfields programs. Examples of such programs are the technical and information workshops for communities such as the NIEHS Technical Workshop on Environmental Job Training for Inner City Youth at Cuyahoga Community College in Cleveland, Ohio in 1995. Continued support by EPA of NIEHS's Minority Worker Training Program now under pilot operation in a number of Brownfields cities is very important.

• • 6e. Continue to support, and then expand on, significant employment and training models, particularly those that provide youth training and pre-apprenticeship opportunities such as urban forestry and agriculture projects.

• • 6f. Target labor unions and faith groups as key partners in job training because of their direct ties to the communities and their significant training infrastructures.

• • 6g. Initiate a series of job summit to define local trends and job opportunities within Brownfields communities.

• • 6h. Provide support for developing ventures in pollution prevention, materials reuse and recycling, environmental cleanup, and related areas.

• • 6i. Increase research on job market opportunities related to urban revitalization and environmental cleanup.

7. *Land Use*

Past land use decisions, many of which are socially inequitable and racially discriminatory, are a major contributor to the inequitable distribution of the burdens and benefits of modern industrial society. Public Dialogue participants cited numerous accounts of the placement of polluting industries that produce toxic chemicals in area where people live, work, play, and go to school.

Participants insisted that Brownfields initiatives must examine the relationship between past, current, and future land use. In particular, they were clear that decisions about future land use must be rooted in community-led processes. They contrasted the community-driven approach with corporate liability-driven proposals which, under the guise of a future industrial land use designation, clean up sites to levels inadequate to protect public health. Such decisions, without the participation or leadership of community residents who have already suffered from the prior pollution of their neighborhood, merely turns these communities into sacrifice areas. The recommendations on enhanced community participation cited in earlier sections of this report must also be applied to land use policies and decision-making.

> *"One baseline issue is community control over land use. The whole process of land use, and control over zoning and development, is really at the core of how many of our communities got to the place that they are in now. Perhaps it is a way by which they can work their way out of the situation… Many of our communities--it's across the board in most low income communities of color--are often zoned for mixed-use. So we have industrial, commercial and residential development in the places where we live.*
>
> *AWe have a situation in New York where two incredibly different communities exist in one local zoning area, i.e., West Harlem, where I live, and Morningside Heights, where Columbia University is located. West Harlem is zoned mixed-use. We have sewage treatment plants, bus depots, chemical waste storage centers, transportation routes (including one for hazardous wastes). All of that criss-crosses each other every day right through our community, and we're surrounded by highways on three sides. But in the Morningside Heights community, which is the southern neighbor of our community, you cannot so much as zone a newsstand without going through incredible land use regulations to get any kind of land use that is not residentially zoned.*
>
> *"I sit on the local zoning board. It's become clear to me that if we don't get involved in that process, we are never going to understand it or perhaps, change it in a way that really respects the interests of local communities. We have gotten a lot better at being able to identify how issues of environmental justice, urban revitalization, economic redevelopment, and land use are intimately connected. You really can't think about one without the other."*
>
> Vernice Miller
> Northeast Environmental Justice Network
> Boston, MA, Public Dialogue

Most citizens working on urban revitalization issues from a community-based perspective take it as a given that decisions about land use, and increased community participation in land use decisions, are an integral part of urban revitalization and appropriate Brownfields redevelopment. Few would deny that zoning practices and lending practices, such as redlining, have a strong historical role in racial discrimination and have led to lower land values in many economically distressed areas. It is only logical that reversing these past abuses must be a critical part of revitalizing these areas. Further, any multi-stakeholder attempts to improve the conditions of distressed and under-utilized areas (particularly involving state and federal policies) must not be countered by future local land use policies that are not coordinated with the overarching urban revitalization strategy. As noted earlier, Brownfields redevelopment must be linked to help address the broader set of community goals and needs, including residential retention and other efforts to ensure the long-term survivability of current communities.

Participants also expressed concerned that Brownfields proposals may become a means for justifying levels of clean-up based upon planned future land use that are not fully protective of public health. They were clear that the voices of residents in a polluted area should be the primary determinant of acceptable levels of clean-up. Those who claim that the community will always require the maximum level of clean-up, ignore the fact that, far better than anyone else, the community recognizes the dangers of losing any cleanup by demanding a full cleanup. Urban revitalization may demand compromises, but these compromises must be supported by those who bear the burdens of incomplete cleanup. Those who bear the burdens of incomplete clean-up must also receive direct benefits from revitalization as opposed to only the indirect benefits of an improved tax base and jobs often filled by non-residents who leave only their car exhaust when commuting to the newly created jobs.

Ultimately, elected officials, policy makers, and the governmental bureaucracy must recognize there is a difference from the sometimes necessary option of limiting future land use because cleanup is not feasible and the undesirable option of allowing the polluter to limit the level of cleanup to reduce the cost of cleanup.

Participants repeatedly described the inadequacy of zoning and facility siting procedures to provide comprehensive, timely, and understandable information about the impacts of new and existing facilities on communities. Without such information, the community can have no meaningful voice in land use decisions directly affecting their lives. Far too often, potentially polluting development is permitted without regard to cumulative impacts on the community.

Land use planning has, and will be, a function of local government, but Federal and State governments have an important role to play in facilitating equitable, environmentally sound land use planning. Dialogue participants were impressed with the capacity of LandView II to combine the expertise of Federal, State, and local governments and community member resources to track the accumulation of pollutants. Easy access to this information empowers the community to better impact the location of polluting sources and to seek mechanisms for pollution reduction within the community.

Several participants stressed the need to replace highly polluting sources with better operations and technology. Others proposed strategic placement of polluting sources together where their regulatory compliance could be monitored and their impacts separated from residential and sensitive populations. Most participants encouraged development of "green businesses" in urban areas, and some also noted the need for more deliberative planning for the "non-green" businesses that comprise much of current manufacturing and development. Non-green businesses should operate in a more environmentally protective manner and in areas with well-planned transportation and limited exposure to residents. Finally, Dialogue participants noted the wisdom of acting now to provide small but incrementally beneficial enhancements to land use- urban farms, nature trails, green spaces, and other conservation projects.

Participants called for an approach to land use based upon principles of **equity**. They called for a holistic examination of equity issues which looks at social justice and economic distribution issues throughout the entire metropolitan area surrounding Brownfields.

A regional approach is essential to understanding these issues. Brownfields sites will always be in competition with Greenfields areas for development. Regardless of improvements of the environmental liability conditions of an urban site, issues such as public safety, decaying infrastructure, and lack of social amenities must be addressed as well. The health of center city areas is crucial to the future health of suburban areas. Government can play a positive role by providing opportunities for discussion of the common interests of urban, suburban, and exurban areas. Land use planning and zoning decisions should be rationalized with a regional perspective. While local political subdivisions may feel they are in competition for economic development and may differ over decisions on encouraging development in under-utilized urban areas or controlling growth in Greenfields areas, this lack of agreement should not be allowed to undercut discussion and reasoned debate. There is a need for at least discussion and understanding of the issues involved even if agreement or shared planning is difficult to achieve.

Disinvestment can be driven by subsidies provided for industrial development in Greenfields areas. Our society and government policies have a bias toward Greenfields development. These subsidies can take the form of government built infrastructure such as roads, water and sewerage. It can come in the form of direct subsidies through tax abatements.

Finding common interests between urban, suburban, and exurban residents will be a key to addressing these issues. Rural interest in retaining their small town character, suburban interest in holding back the congestion that drove them away from the urban center, and the inner city's desire for redevelopment can form the basis of a common interest. Though the issues of urban economic plight, suburban congestion, and the loss of farm and wilderness lands are different problems, they each share a common solution as an alternative to Greenfields development. Forums which explore the common concerns and common solutions to these problems will build a broader constituency for Brownfields initiatives.

SPECIFIC RECOMMENDATIONS:

7-1. *Examine land use patterns of an entire metropolitan area or region surrounding Brownfields sites.*

Brownfields do not exist in a vacuum. Activities formerly in these areas often have not simply ceased to exist, but moved to other areas. New development must choose between locating in Brownfields communities and Greenfields areas. If the perception exists that Greenfields are the place to invest due to various amenities there and the disamenities in urban areas, it will be difficult to attract development regardless of what is done to enhance a Brownfields area. If government is in fact subsidizing Greenfields development, it may become impossible to attract outside capital.

7-2. *Identify natural advantages of Brownfields areas.*

Industry originally was built in urban centers and Brownfields areas because of natural advantages such as access to water, transportation, or natural features. Additional infrastructure such as sewerage, universities, and transportation links were built around these industrial centers and often remain. In addition, these areas often are less susceptible to natural disasters. These natural advantages must be identified, chronicled and disseminated to improve perceptions of these areas.

If the real costs of new roads, new sewage systems, increased automobile traffic, and other financial burdens of Greenfields development were incorporated into developer costs or not subsidized by the government, Brownfields areas would be more competitive. The playing field between Brownfields sites and Greenfields sites actually may be level when natural advantages of the urban core are taken into account. The playing field may actually be fair if Greenfields development is not subsidized.

7-3. *Encourage and support the involvement of non-traditional stakeholders (such as community-based organizations) in government processes, such as zoning issues.*

Government officials should be accountable for not only providing "opportunities" for public input but, in making a good faith effort to succeed in securing public input, it is not enough to simply hold a meeting or provide opportunities for access. Government officials must make an effort to achieve meaningful public participation through long-term consistent interaction with community-based organizations and institutions. Educating the public about basic decision-making processes that determine development and zoning patterns will result in stronger democratic processes, greater public participation, and better decision making for the public as a whole.

7-4. *Encourage investment in degraded urban environments by supporting and integrating activities to improve public safety access to health care, schools, and other social factors that may limit investment even after cleanup.*

This can take the form of linking federal grants from other agencies to Brownfields grants in communities. Community-based groups working on broader social justice problems can be educated and supported on environmental problems and solutions through urban redevelopment. Federal programs such as AmeriCorps, already focus on environment and public safety as separate areas. How can they be joined? Programs such as the Empowerment and Enterprise zones can bring far more resources to bear on the same communities and problems than can the Brownfields initiatives on their own.

7-5. *Explore the linkages between U.S. government international trade policies, disinvestment in urban areas, and reinvestment in Greenfields sites.*

U.S. trade policies and commitment to free trade have reduced barriers to existing U.S. companies moving to other countries in search of cheap labor. In theory, the dropping of these barriers and the creation of new markets for U.S. products purchased by newly hired workers will result in a new gain in hobs and economic activity in our country. It is likely the plants that close are disproportionately older plants located in Brownfields areas while the new U.S. plants built to serve new markets are located in Greenfields areas. Although U.S. trade policy is designed to bring about a net benefit for the country as a whole, it will be necessary to assess where these benefits and losses occur and steps be taken to level the playing field.

7-6. Urge cities, states, tribal and territorial governments to review their planning and land use review and permitting processes to address environmental justice issues, such as environmental health, cumulative risk, and incompatible mixed land uses; offer assistance to local governments for incorporating public participation and accountability in formulating policies and plans and in local decision-making.

---

7. ACTION ITEMS

- • 7a. Convene dialogues on land use planning between political subdivisions in the regions in which Brownfields sites are located.

- • 7b. Identify the real costs of Greenfields development.

- • 7c. Support and encourage interaction of stakeholders from communities in urban, suburban, and exurban areas.

- • 7d. Link Brownfields with transportation infrastructure development, particularly those related to mass transit (see experiences of this critical link in communities such as Bayview Hunters Point in San Francisco, California; the Green Line in Chicago, Illinois; and Fruitvale, California).

- • 7e. Maximize the use of LandView II and other mapping tools to integrate landuse planning and environmental protection.

- • 7f. Dedicate resources to expanding and updating the databases used by LandView II and other mapping tools, including:

  - •• All environmental permits under federal, state or local authorities
  - •• Criteria for identifying potential sources of pollution exempt from regulatory obligations
  - •• Hazardous waste contamination and toxic releases

- • 7g. Assist communities in the compilation of their own data, including, providing advice on tracking, preparing guidelines for organizing data, identifying common sources of lead and asbestos, providing a means of discovering and deterring illegal dumping, among others.

III. **PUBLIC AND PRIVATE SECTOR PARTNERSHIPS**

8. *Community/Private Sector Partnerships*

At the root of the problems confronting urban/Brownfields communities are massive economic shifts that have marked the past two decades. Hundreds of thousands of industrial jobs have either disappeared or moved away from the central city and its neighborhoods. While some downtown areas have experienced revival, the jobs created are very different than those which once sustained neighborhoods. For many people in older city neighborhoods, new approaches to rebuilding their lives and communities, new openings to opportunities, are a vital necessity.

In looking at barriers to reinvestment and revitalization, the Brownfields Initiative must look at non-environmental barriers such as high taxes, depressed property values, crime, congestion, redlining, level of community services, and racial discrimination in lending and insurance practices. Among these is environmental contamination--both past and present.

The Public Dialogues sought to engage all institutions about their roles in ensuring healthy and sustainable communities. The Subcommittee took the position that all social institutions--including faith groups, labor unions, universities, philanthropies, business, and others--have a responsibility to participate in a meaningful way in achieving urban revitalization and building healthy and sustainable communities. Their participation should be consistent with community

> *"Our vision is of an urban village working cooperatively to improve the quality of life and conditions of our neighborhoods with an emphasis on sustainable development that is economically and ecologically sound. We seek to empower and inspire members of our neighborhoods, especially our children and youth, to develop effective responses to the needs of our communities and to promote cooperation, collaboration, and partnership with social service agencies, governments, and the private sector to create liveable communities. We seek to positively impact the social, economic, and spiritual development of our neighborhood and cities. A priority of our Zone is providing safe, decent, and affordable housing. Our vision can become a reality when our community becomes a cooperative village, an extended family that is self-reliant, self-sufficient, and self determined...I think that's one of the most beautiful vision [statements] I have had the opportunity to hear and take part in developing. It is the vision of the Atlanta Empowerment Zone Community."*
>
> Sulaiman Madhi
> Atlanta Summit Against Poverty
> Atlanta, GA, Public Dialogue

> *"I heard a lot of discussion about involvement and partnership. That's certainly the direction we have to take. But I would suggest taking it one step farther. The community actually has to take charge. It seems to me that if you look at the environmental justice movement, it started with an awakening--a realization that there was a lot of pollution that was victimizing the people living there. The second stage was kind of a reaction stage where people said 'don't put it here; if you want to put a new incinerator up, don't put it here--we have had enough pollution.' Based on what I heard this morning, I suggest that it's time now for communities to actually take charge to create a vision of what they want for their communities, to work with their local government, to make it competitive for somebody to invest that kind of business in that location."*
>
> Richard Morrison
> Bank of America
> Oakland, CA, Public Dialogue

> *"My father came from the south, [where he worked] as a sharecropper. He got a job in the auto industry, with the UAW. He did not have the education but he had the drive. Because of that, he was able to make a living for himself...Today, our generation does not have the same opportunities. I have several degrees and I'm working in a voluntary capacity. What we are seeing is a lot of frustration, a lot of frustration and anger. These things definitely need to be addressed.*
>
> Derrick Willis
> Emmanuel Community Center
> Detroit, MI, Public Dialogue

empowerment principles. This involves a commitment of real resources--human and financial--for accomplishing the task.

Many participants commented that the Brownfields Initiative must build partnerships not only between community and government agencies, but with other groups and institutions who can assist with urban revitalization. These partnerships are essential to solving problems which are difficult for one entity to address alone. The importance of forging partnerships with youth through schools and other communities was reiterated; young people within a community who possess leadership capabilities can be the solution to many problems. Partnerships must bring all stakeholders to the table as equal partners.

Much distrust of corporations and the business sector exists in communities, especially in places like South Central Los Angeles and Detroit where residents have witnessed a history of corporate disinvestment. However, members of the business community affirmed the importance of an empowered community and the need for forthright dialogue. This could go a long way toward bridging the current gap between community-based planning models and a commitment from developers, industry, and business to better understand and support use of such approaches. Matching worthy community-driven projects with adequate financial resources is a challenge of paramount importance.

Realistically, all parties to community-based planning need to recognize that finding willing developers and investors are key components to redeveloping Brownfields. In many cases, developers have a particular project or proposal in mind as their reason for acquiring property and initiating the redevelopment process. In these situations, the authors of this report urge that developers (and regulators involved in the process) involve communities early in the planning process. Early community participation can ensure that the design and implementation of redevelopment activities are consistent with community goals. In other cases, communities have crafted well-defined visions for their redevelopment and will need to find developers and investors willing to finance such redevelopment. In these cases, regulators should use available resources to facilitate this process.

The Subcommittee is mindful of the fact that EPA's Brownfields Initiative is only a small beginning. It provides resources only for planning, assessment, and partnership building. None of present Brownfields Pilot Project funding goes to actual site cleanup or job training activities. This has been a source of great consternation for the many community groups who are interested in initiating projects around specific Brownfields sites. Nonetheless these funds have played a invaluable role in getting the process started. There also are heartening examples of significant funds being leveraged as a result of the Brownfields Pilot Projects.

Government agencies and societal institutions must not view communities as merely an assortment of needs but as a collection of assets which can be built upon. Great resilience exists in the economic, cultural, and spiritual life of America's communities. There exists many stellar accomplishments, entrepreneurial successes, and significant victories. Efforts must be made to ensure proper media coverage of these authentic signs of hope.

SPECIFIC RECOMMENDATIONS:

8-1. ***Support efforts to build upon community assets and increase community capacity through information, training, and grassroots organizational development.***

8-2. ***Support community efforts to identify and mobilize institutional resources for community revitalization.***

8-3. ***Support community efforts to press financial institutions to become more responsive to their concerns, particularly through mechanisms like the Community Reinvestment Act.***

*8-4. **Strengthen partnerships between communities and academic institutions as part of efforts to help communities achieve the skills necessary for self-advocacy, increase access to information, and provide a forum for the exchange and testing of innovative ideas.***

*8-5. **Coordinate with philanthropic groups to provide resources to community groups for technical assistance and other needs.***

*8-6. **Promote partnerships between local businesses and the communities where firms are based, including use of community advisory panels.***

*8-7. **Encourage mechanisms to bring together Chambers of Commerce, community groups, and local planning authorities to share information about revitalization and redevelopment goals.***

*8-8. **Encourage suburban residents to participate in, and contribute to, urban revitalization efforts.***

*8-9. **Invite local groups, faith groups, labor organizations, schools, philanthropies and others to play a role in bringing together multiple stakeholders, amplifying the voice of the community, and supporting community volunteer staff who are spread thin with a myriad of commitments.***

---

8. ACTION ITEMS

- • 8a. Institute a Brownfields small grants program (perhaps modeled after the EPA Environmental Justice Small Grants Program) to fund local community groups for the purposes of conducting community education, leadership development, and technical assistance.

- • 8b. Convene a National Urban Brownfields Summit Meeting of all stakeholders working on, or affected by, Brownfields projects as an opportunity to bring together all parties to discuss critical issues, craft unified strategies, and determine actions for follow-up.

- • 8c. Develop educational curriculum for schools that encourages student interest in reclaiming their environment and other ways of developing partnerships with the local educational system-- public and private.

- • 8d. Assign staff to work in local groups, universities, and local governments in partnership with local communities.

- • 8e. Support efforts to establish local-based environmental roundtables dedicated to addressing issues of achieving healthy and sustainable communities, including environmental justice, public health, Brownfields, land use planning, residential retention, and other issues.

- • 8f. Support the establishment of a National Urban Revitalization and Brownfields Training Institute to develop and implement training programs for achieving healthy and sustainable communities.

---

9. **Local, State, Tribal, and Territorial Governments**

The role of local, state, tribal, and territorial Governments in urban revitalization/ Brownfields issues is an area of great importance. This is particularly true since the Brownfields issue ultimately revolves around voluntary cleanup. Local, state, tribal, and territorial governments each play unique roles and have specific needs. The Subcommittee urges that much attention be given to this area.

Local governments increasingly recognize the importance of addressing contaminated properties and Brownfields issues. Mature urbanized areas are now faced with a second or third generation of development. Properties must be reclaimed and reused if these cities are to remain prosperous. Municipalities are beset with the effects of economic disinvestment job loss, and tax base depletion as well as the negative impacts of urban sprawl and resultant vehicular traffic, congestion, air pollution, and energy waste.

There is no doubt that all municipalities critically need to find tangible solutions to the problems represented by urban decay and the presence of Brownfields sites. These are enormous challenges because:

•• Municipalities often lack the technical expertise on the regulatory and legal details of the Brownfields problems and require assistance in building capacity.

•• Municipalities often lack the means to capitalize upon and promote new opportunities for local job creation and business development, particularly in inner city neighborhoods, through training, technical, and financial assistance.

•• Municipalities often lack the capacity to identify and develop new and innovative financing strategies.

•• Municipalities often lack adequate mechanisms for ensuring full participation of the community and other stakeholders

•• Municipalities are themselves often beset with difficult to resolve liability problems.

In short, the vast majority of local governments lack the capacity and resources to develop effective strategies for dealing with the multitude of Brownfields within their jurisdiction. Local governments must be empowered to find a radically different approach to solving urban revitalization/Brownfields problems; this entails full involvement of impacted communities, new partnerships, and adequate resources.

In the eyes of many State governments, Brownfields redevelopment is an exciting initiative because it allows us to envision the passage of unused, polluted real estate through a sound environmental cleanup, and culminate to a usable property which can make a difference in peoples' lives. Such a process must, at an early stage, pass through a successful environmental cleanup in order to proceed on to an outcome where the real value to people is achievable. If the cleanup is delayed or impaired, the whole project would suffer. States request that it be understood that regulatory management and oversight at any specific Brownfields site will not be provided by the federal government but by the State voluntary cleanup program office. Because virtually no potential Brownfields sites are on the National Priorities List, the federal government's direct involvement in actual site cleanup may be minimal. Thus, if too few participants understand that there is a key state role to be executed at a critical early nexus of the Brownfields process, i.e., the execution of a sound cleanup, there is danger that delays could result from a lack of early communications with state voluntary program offices regarding coordination, early identification of acceptable remedies, and arrangements to meet state cleanup standards and procedures.

American Indians, Alaskan Natives, and other indigenous peoples have a unique cultural and legal relationship to the United States that deserve special consideration. Despite federal agency mandates to fulfill the trust responsibility to Tribes that reflect the government-to-government relationship, Tribes have not been treated equitably compared to states. As a result, many Tribes do not have environmental infrastructures to stop degradation of the environment and remediate environmental damage. These lands, which are among the most impoverished in the nation, are subjected to a broad range of environmental problems including illegal dumping, hazardous waste disposal, surface and groundwater contamination, air pollution, leaking underground and above ground storage tanks, military pollution and threats, mining wastes, habitat destruction and human health risks. Inadequate funding from the Federal government has led to many environmental problems which tribes face today. Environmental justice with tribes must assure the right of tribes to protect, regulate and manage their environmental resources.

In addition, there are special concerns for Native Americans who have been relocated to urban areas and who are no longer functioning within tribal government jurisdiction. The Federal responsibility for the well-being of these individuals is not limited to the boundaries of tribal lands. Accordingly, it is important for EPA and other agencies with such responsibilities to assure that urban revitalization programs provide appropriate participation and visibility for this group of community concerns.

Another area deserving of special attention are Brownfields issues in U.S. Territories. For example, Brownfields sites may exist in significant numbers in Puerto Rico. Moreover, the Subcommittee believes that territories are similar to American Indian Tribes in terms of their environmental infrastructure needs.

The present Brownfields pilot projects are totally dependent on full participation of local, state, tribal, and territorial Governments for planning and implementation activities. Under existing law EPA looks to state, local, tribal, and territorial governments as the legal operating entity for the implementation of Brownfields program grants. Because these entities are the receiving source of funds it is clear that they are the principal organizations which must form the community partnerships that will enable successful Brownfields programs to come into fruition. Moreover, as the governmental entities where the affected communities are located, the participation of the local, state, tribal, and/or territorial government is essential to the effective outcome of any urban revitalization/Brownfields strategy.

Unfortunately there is much evidence of lack of communications and distrust between government organizations and communities concerned with the Brownfields programs. The Subcommittee found during its hearings that this distrust is not in the distant past, but is a continuing barrier to EPA's effective implementation of this program. How to bring the various community interests together with the necessary operating government officials was a recurring theme of all the Public Dialogues, and to a certain extent, the dominant theme at more than one of them. Since the government organizations, or some other entity created by them will the moving force behind urban cleanup efforts, it is a serious challenge to design a protocol that will move beyond the lack of communications and distrust into meaningful communications and positive action by all the concerned parties.

SPECIFIC RECOMMENDATIONS:

9-1. *Improve coordination between and among multiple levels of government (federal, state, local, tribal, and territorial) to enable an integrated approach to Brownfields as part of overall community revitalization efforts.*

9-2. *Collaborate with local, state, tribal, and territorial governments to streamline, consolidate, and provide predictability in Brownfields regulations, while assuring full protection of public health and the environment.*

9-3. *Support and develop strategies to finance local cleanup, including direct funding, incentives, private sector investment, and innovative public financing.*

9-4. *Assist local governments to identify and target environmentally sound industries and incorporate pollution prevention in Brownfields redevelopment projects.*

9-5. ***Work with local governments to promote community-based environmental protection.***

---

9. ACTION ITEMS

- • 9a. Support pilot projects to local, state, tribal, and territorial governments that foster and integrate community involvement in Brownfields redevelopment and target sustainable jobs for the local community.

- • 9b. Assist communities in applying for Brownfields assistance programs to achieve early coordination with state and local cleanup agencies who will oversee the actual cleanup at non-NPL sites.

- • 9c. Work with local, state, tribal, and territorial governments to build capacity to address Brownfields issues, through enhanced technical assistance, staff exchanges through the Intergovernmental Personnel Act (IPA), training, and pilot projects.

- • 9d. Specify a requirement in federal grants and other assistance to parties engaged in arranging site cleanups under the federal Brownfields assistance to comply with all applicable state and local statutes and regulations in conducting that cleanup.

- • 9e. Provide training environmental justice issues are considred in federally-supported programs and grants, such as the Empowerment and Enterprise Zone programs, block grants, and restoration of federal facilities.

- • 9f. Ensure that environmental justice issues are considered in federally-supported programs and grants, such as the Empowerment and Enterprise Zone programs, block grants, and restoration of federal facilities.

- • 9g. Develop a Brownfields grants program specifically designed to meet the special needs of Native American Tribes and U.S. Territories.

---

10. *Federal Interagency Cooperation, Programmatic Integration, and Government Reinvention*

The original and most enduring proponents of government reinvention are community residents engaged in overcoming systemic impediments to locally-based solutions. A resounding theme of the Public Dialogues was the need for federal interagency cooperation and coordination. Different federal programs must be integrated in the context of problems defined by the community. By definition, genuine government reinvention cannot take place unless it is a community-driven process.

The heart and soul of an authentic government reinvention process is the many vibrant and coherent community-based visions of healthy and sustainable communities. The Public Dialogues illustrated this fact must be applied to issues of the role of different federal agencies. Communities begin with a holistic understanding of their history, needs, assets, and aspirations. They see issues such as consideredup sites, creating jobs, ensuring decent housing, ensuring investment and economic development, and ending the debilitating effect of racism as cross-cutting and inseparable issues. Such community-based visions provide the compass for public policy discourse on the role of the federal government and government restructuring.

There already exists many federal policy and program initiatives which lend themselves to viable integrative strategies. These include EPA's "targeted geographic initiatives" and "community-based environmental protection," HUD's "empowerment zones/enterprise communities" and "livable cities," DOT's "livable communities," and CDC's "healthy homes, healthy communities, and healthy peoples" concepts. Similar such policy and program initiatives exist in literally every federal agency seriously attempting to address place-based, multi-faceted, and cross-cutting issues such as urban revitalization and Brownfields.

> *"I want to introduce into the record a paper recently published on collaborative processes for community improvement. It can easily be applied to the Brownfields question. The author speaks to the need for articulating the role of the community as the central initiator and guider in the process. He argues that we have a number of interactions between federal government, local governments, academic institutions, and communities. Many of us do networking on a regular basis. But there is a higher level of interacting called coordination, i.e., trying to work across federal agencies and do some planning together. There is a next level called cooperation, e.g., perhaps setting budget priorities in more thoughtful and flexible ways. The paper advances the idea of an entire level of interaction called collaborative empowerment. This is something new; it gets to the heart of some of the debates about environmental justice.*
>
> *"The communities who are grappling with disproportionate impacts on their environment, their health, and their future, must be the organizations that set the goals and objectives as to what will occur in their communities. Those of us--be it from federal agencies, academic institutions, foundations, or otherwise--need to interact from the position of helping to evolve those goals into a larger empowerment and betterment mode. After the communities have established goals and objectives, it is time for sitting down, doing an analysis of the available pool of resources, and how they will bring these resources to the table in a way that elevates the contribution of the community itself.*
>
> *"This paper argues that the first element of community-based goal setting is a discussion about values... This is not often a starting point for discussions about environmental health research, but I do believe there are hopeful signs for the future in this arena. The first is the [Federal] Interagency Working Group on Environmental Justice Task Force for Model Projects. One of the mandatory characteristic of a project is to seek involvement of representatives from adversely impacted populations in all phases of the projects--[from] initiation, design, conduct, and [through] evaluation. We have not yet implemented these mandatory characteristics in all models of our interagency projects. But I think the principle is available for everybody to challenge the federal government on."*
>
> Gerry Poje
> **National Institute for Environmental Health Sciences**
> **Atlanta, GA, Public Dialogue**

Executive Order 12898 on environmental justice presents a logical opportunity to begin that process. For this reason, the NEJAC adopted a resolution calling upon EPA to:

•*request that the development of one unified, integrated, and cross-cutting strategy to address issues of urban revitalization and the development of healthy and sustainable communities be made a priority agenda item for the implementation of Executive Order 12898 and the Interagency Working Group on Environmental Justice.*[22]*"*

In addition, the Subcommittee sees great value in interfacing with the Federal Facility Environmental Restoration Dialogue Committee (FFERDC). In December 1995, the Subcommittee began a formal dialogue with members of FFERDC. We believe that the federal facilities cleanup process has developed many lessons which apply directly to the Brownfields Initiative. There is an entire body of protocols and knowledge about community participation, environmental cleanup, and ecological restoration issues developed as a result of this process.[23] Moreover, there are linkages between federal facility cleanup, urban revitalization, and Brownfields which must be tapped to achieve the full societal benefit of these programs. We believe that similar processes should be taking place with other federal agencies and initiatives as well.

The urban crisis--in which Brownfields issues are embedded-- is systemic in nature. Efforts to resolve any single problem are doomed to failure if they are not integrated into a multi-faceted strategy. Government must be reinvented to address this reality. Government reinvention cannot merely be talk. The American electorate is absolutely correct in rejecting wastefulness, inefficiency, and bureaucratic insensitivity. However this does not mean that they are adverse to making sound investments for a better future. They demand decision making processes which have integrity and to which they are connected. There exists widespread anxiety about our common future and people seek authentic signs of hope.

EPA and other federal agencies must be committed to developing a unified set of strategies which will provide an authentic sign of hope and thus prove capable of imbuing the American people with a sense of a new ennobling nation mission. The Subcommittee posed the following question: What is the importance of having a coherent, unified, multi-faceted, and energizing urban revitalization strategy which can provide an anchor for mobilization of non-governmental resources?

SPECIFIC RECOMMENDATIONS:

10-1. *Develop a strategy to coalesce a unified federal strategy consisting of all relevant federal agencies to meet the challenge of revitalizing urban America.*

10-2. *Ensure that leadership of all federal agencies visibly project the importance of interagency cooperation and coordination, with a strong message about the overarching importance of interagency coordination and cooperation. Given the cross-cutting and interrelated nature of the urban crisis, the success of urban revitalization, Brownfields and other initiatives are dependant for their success on the fullest possible interagency cooperation and coordination. Given the understanding anxiety these issues cause for federal agency staff, strong leadership must be come from the top on the need for reinventing government.*

10-3. *Provide opportunities for communities to systematically engage EPA and other federal agencies in ways in which they can coordinate programs, pool resources, and tap into expertise.*

10-4. *Utilize Executive Order 12898 on environmental justice and the Federal Interagency Working Group on Environmental Justice as a mechanism to build partnerships and to coalesce a unified national strategy across all federal agencies.*

10-5. *Ensure programmatic integration between Brownfields and other EPA programs. Integrate place-based approaches to environmental protection with sector-based approaches and their implications for industrial policy.*

*10-6. **Establish a Working Group that specifically consists of federal agencies that have Indian Programs and Indian mandates. This working group could be part of the Interagency Working Group on Environmental Justice.***

*10-7. **Recognize in all key issues and recommendations the requirements outlined in Presidential Executive Order No. 12???, issued May 24, 1996, which promotes accommodation of access to Native American sacred sites by Indian religious practitioners and provides additional protection for the physical integrity of such sites.***

---

10. ACTION ITEMS

• • 10a. Compile an inventory of all federal policy and program initiatives which are relevant to urban revitalization and Brownfields; such an inventory can serve as a road-map for communities.

• • 10b. Build a series of bi-lateral partnerships such that together they achieve a critical mass for coalescing a unified strategy capable of tapping multiple resources and expertise; partners should include DOT, HUD, DoD, DOE, HHS, Centers for Disease Control, NIEHS, the Federal Deposit Insurance Corporation, DOL, the Occupational Health and Safety Administration, the National Institutes for Occupational Safety and Health, the Economic Development Administration, DOI, DOJ, DOA, and the U.S. Department of Education.

• • 10c. Form partnerships to work in an interagency manner on regional and local levels, particularly in Brownfields pilot project cities--support •one stop shopping• at the community level for all federal agencies.

• • 10d. Establish an interagency task force on urban revitalization and Brownfields redevelopment, working through either the Interagency Working Group on Environmental Justice (EWG) or other appropriate mechanisms.

CONCLUSION

> •*The future of its cities may well decide America's survival not merely as a society but as a civilization. As we look to the 21st century, what endeavor could possibly be more eminently worthy and necessary; more obviously logical and deserving of our national attention, expertise, and resources; or more meaningful and spiritually nourishing than that of revitalizing America's urban areas and ensuring healthy and sustainable communities--both urban and rural. A challenge so great as this cannot be met without compelling visions of what constitutes healthy and sustainable communities. We have found that such visions already exist in highly coherent and vibrant ways within many communities across the nation.*••
>
> *Charles Lee*
> *United Church of Christ Commission for Racial Justice*

Brownfields are inseparable from environmental justice and urban revitalization. When put into proper context, they reveal a nexus of issues which are indeed civilizational in dimension. Without just and livable, environmentally sound, economically sustainable, spiritually and psychologically whole urban communities, the ecological integrity of all areas in the nation--if not the world--is jeopardized. To achieve healthy and sustainable urban communities, we cannot evade the multitude of issues raised through the Brownfields debate.

A host of issues are associated with the systemic crisis in America's urban centers. In the fullest sense the urban crisis is fundamentally an ecological one, rooted in among other things the racial makeup of the structure of American cities. These issues include the untenable growth of urban sprawl, ecological importance of the urban environment, the vexing issues of race in American society, new frontiers for conduct of environmental science, reinventing government, the displacement of residents thorugh gentrification of exisiting communities, building of new partnerships between, and new community-driven visions of revitalization that properly balance economic and environmental choices.

The Subcommittee believes that these are issues we as a nation can ill afford to ignore. We saw the Public Dialogues on "Urban Revitalization and Brownfields: Envisioning Healthy and Sustainable Communities" as an attempt to stimulate a new and vigorous public discourse over the environmental and economic future of America's cities. We hope that these Public Dialogues are only the beginning of many efforts by which solutions to urban revitalization/Brownfields issues can be coalesced into a coherent and compelling social vision.

The nation is locked within the throes of a set of transitions which are demographic, economic, environmental, technological, social, cultural, linguistic, generational, and indeed spiritual in nature. Urban revitalization and Brownfields offer an opportunity to shape new policy, programs, partnerships, and pilot projects which rise to the challenge of the cross-cutting issues raised in this report. The Subcommittee continues to pose these questions:

•• Can this process begin to set a direction capable of crystallizing a unifying and cross-cutting vision within the federal government to serve as an anchor for the mobilization of society's resources--both public and private?

•• Can the restoration of the physical environment in America's cities become the anchoring point for economic, social, cultural, and spiritual renewal and thus provide the basis for embarking upon a new and ennobling national mission?

As we confront the next century, the nation desperately needs a vision which will address issues of racial and economic polarization, economic and ecological sustainability, full mobilization of both public and private sector resources, and the capacity to engage in meaningful public discourse. As many Public Dialogue participants reiterated, "These are indeed issues of civilizational dimensions."

In order to translate the momentum, enthusiasm, and hard work already committed to this issue into tangible and lasting benefits, EPA and other federal agencies must begin to think about a new framework which will address the issues raised through the Public Dialogues. The hallmark of that process must be informed and empowered community involvement. At the same time, the Subcommittee recommends that all agencies in the federal government consider the cross-cutting issues raised in the report and begin to shape coordinated and integrative strategies. We sincerely thank EPA for its support of the NEJAC Public Dialogues on Urban Revitalization and Brownfields. We hope that it has provided a context as well as a "road map" for moving in such a direction.

Envisioning the Next Phase of Urban Revitalization

As we look to the 21st century, what endeavor could possibly be more eminently worthy and necessary; more obviously logical and deserving of our national attention, expertise, and resources; or more meaningful and spiritually nourishing than that of revitalizing America's urban areas and ensuring healthy and sustainable communities, both urban and rural? A challenge so great as this cannot be met with compelling visions of what constitutes healthy and sustainable communities. We have found that such visions already exist in highly coherent and vibrant ways within many communities across the nation.

The questions outlined above form the guiding elements for envisioning the next phase of urban revitalization/Brownfields strategies. The NEJAC Subcommittee felt the need to identify priorities for the next two to four years from the above recommendations. The Subcommittee recognized that the Brownfields Initiative has achieve broad based support because it linked two critical areas, i.e., environmental cleanup with job creation. Over the past year, the Subcommittee has worked to stimulate dialogue on ensuring the following issue linkages:

• • Environmental cleanup with job creation

• • Federal facilities cleanup and restoration with urban revitalization/Brownfields

• • Urban revitalization/Brownfields with transportation, regional land use, and the Department of Transportation's "Livable Communities" Initiative

•• Ensuring the long-term surviviblility of existing communities

• • Urban revitalization/Brownfields, public health, and community-based planning

We believe that a maturing discussion on the above issues will take place over the next year and provide the catalyst for a unified federal approach towards coalescing a common urban revitalization strategy across all federal agencies. Several other priorities must take place over the next two to four years:

• • Establish an interagency urban revitalization/Brownfields task force, either through Federal Interagency Working Group on Environmental Justice or other appropriate mechanism;
• • Convene a National Urban Revitalization/Brownfields Summit (this should be portrayed as a •national revival• for the cities);
• • Support the establishment of a National Urban Revitalization/Brownfields Training Institute to develop and train in achieving healthy and sustainable communities;
• • Convene a dialogue between community groups and developers/investors to achieve a common framework for decision making and working partnerships;
• • Ensure support for worker training programs and establish mechanisms for better coordination;
• • Establish special grant programs in areas of technical assistance to communities, small grants for community based advocacy and training, and a tribal and territorial Brownfields grant program; and

• • Establish new partnerships above and beyond traditional urban revitalization/Brownfields stakeholders to include community based organizations, youth groups, faith groups, labor groups, civil rights groups, public health groups, and philanthropic organizations.

If the Brownfields issue is nothing else, it was an opportunity for community groups to engage government, developers, and other stakeholders around their vision of what healthy and sustainable communities are. The stakes cannot be greater. EPA must begin to think about a new framework which will address the issues raised through the Public Dialogues on Urban Revitalization and Brownfields. The hallmark of that process must be informed and empowered community involvement. Likewise, all agencies in the federal government should consider these cross-cutting issues and begin to shape coordinated and integrative strategies.

The NEJAC Subcommittee on Waste and Facility Siting believes that a process has been started by which environmental justice advocates and impacted communities have changed the operative definition of the term "Brownfields." This already has translated into some significant changes in the way in which EPA implements the Brownfields Initiative. We hope to engage a process which ultimately will coalesce a new type of environmental and social policy capable of meeting the challenges of revitalizing urban America and restoring ecological balance to the nation. This was our intent. Anything less would have amounted to a failure of leadership, a breaking of faith with communities, and acquiescence to business as usual.

ENDNOTES

1. See *OSWER Environmental Justice Action Agenda, May 1995,* and *OSWER Environmental Justice Accomplishments Report.*

2. Having no context within which to understand it, the term "Brownfields" was sometimes interpreted to mean "fields where 'brown' people live." The intent of the term, as it evolved, was to articulate a visual impact of pollution versus "Greenfields," such as forests and pastures. Such cognitive dissonance illuminates some obvious cultural sensitivities surrounding issues of race, urban development, and gentrification.

3. Alston, Dana (Ed.). *We Speak for Ourselves: Social Justice and Environment.* Washington, DC: The Panos Institute, December 1990.

4. Infrastructure includes "living" development of knowledge base, processes and protocols developed mutually by stakeholder groups in the process of addressing and resolving concrete issues.

5. The Northeast/Midwest Institute, founded in 1977, is an independent, non-profit regional policy center that was created as a research arm of the Northeast/Midwest Congressional Coalition, a bipartisan group of lawmakers focusing on the environmental and economic revitalization of this 18-state region.

6. Bank of America, et.al. *Beyond Sprawl: New Patterns of Growth to Fit the New California,* February 1995.

7. Bullard, Robert D., J Eugene Grigsby III and Charles Lee (Ed.) *Residential Apartheid: The American Legacy.* Los Angeles: UCLA Center for Afro-American Studies, 1994.

8. Gauna, Jeane. Presentation to National Advisory Committee, First National People of Color Environmental Leadership Summit. Washington, DC, May 20, 1991.

9. For example, the field of public health began in the 1800's as a social movement to protest the unsanitary conditions of worker communities during the Industrial Revolution.

10. Harris, Fred and Roger Wilkins (Ed.) *Quiet Riots: Race and Poverty in the United States.* New York: Pantheon Books, 1988

11. Hayes-Bautista, David E., Werner O. Schink, and Jorge Chapa. *The Burden of Support: Young Latinos in an Aging Society.* Stanford, CA: Stanford University Press, 1988.; "America's Changing Colors: What Will the U.S. Be like When Whites Are No Longer the Majority?", *Time Magazine (*April 9, 1990) pp. 28-31.; United Church of Christ. "A Pronouncement on Calling the United Church of Christ To Be A Multiracial and Multicultural Church," Adopted by the United Church of Christ 19th General Synod (St. Louis, Missouri) July 15-20, 1993.

12. Presentation of Teresa Cordova on Community Based Planning to NEJAC Waste and Facility Siting Subcommittee (Atlanta, Georgia, January 17, 1995).

13. Takvorian, Diane (Ed.) *Toxic Free Neighborhoods Community Planning Guide.* San Diego: Environmental Health Coalition, 1993.

14. United Church of Christ Commission for Racial Justice. *Toxic Wastes and Race in the United States: A National Report on the Racial and Socioeconomic Characteristics of Communities Surrounding Hazardous Waste Sites.* New York: United Church of Christ, 1987.

15.   Matsuoka, Martha. *Reintegrating the Flatlands: A Regional Framework for Military Base Conversion in the San Francisco Bay Area.* San Francisco: Urban Habitat Program, April 1995.

16.   U.S. Environmental Protection Agency, *The New Generation of Environmental Protection: A Summary of EPA's Five Year Strategic Plan*, July 1994.

17.   Ferris, Deeohn. "A Call for Justice and Equal Environmental Protection" in Bullard, Robert D. (Ed.) *Unequal Protection: Environmental Justice and Communities of Color.* San Francisco: Sierra Club Books, 1994.

18.   U.S. Environmental Protection Agency, *The New Generation of Environmental Protection: A Summary of EPA's Five Year Strategic Plan*, July 1994.

19.   Bullard, Robert D., quoted in Charles Lee, "Would Martin Luther King Have Become an Environmental Justice Advocate?" U.S. Department of Justice Symposium, "A Dream Deferred: Thirty Years After the Civil Rights Act of 1964," Washington, D.C., November 30, 1994.

20.   Ecology, defined as "that which binds all things together--economically, environmentally, socially, culturally, and spiritually."

21.   Ferris, Deeohn. Percival, et.al. *Environmental Regulation, Law, Science, and Policy: 1995 Supplement.* New York: Little, Brown, and Company, 1995, p. 1.

22.   National Environmental Justice Advisory Council, Resolution on "Environmental Justice and Urban Revitalization." Crystal City, Virginia, July 25-26, 1995.

23.   *Final Report of the Federal Facilities Environmental Restoration Dialogue Committee*, April 1996

APPENDICES

ACKNOWLEDGEMENTS

Special thanks go the individuals who organized the individual Public Dialogues, which took place on the following schedule:

Roxbury Community College (June 5, 1995)
Boston, Massachusetts
Sha-King Alston, Center for Family Work and Community

46th Baptist Church (June 7, 1995)
Philadelphia, Pennsylvania
Maurice Sampson, Institute for Local Self-Reliance
Sam Spofforth, Clean Water Action

Belle Isle Nature Center (June 9, 1995)
Detroit, Michigan
Donelle Wilkins, Detroiters for Environmental Justice
Grace Boggs, Detroiters for Environmental Justice
Guy Williams, Detroiters for Environmental Justice/National Wildlife Federation

Niles Hall, Preservation Park (July 18, 1995)
Oakland, California
Martha Matsuoka, Urban Habitat Program
Romel Pascal, Urban Habitat Program
Lenny Siegel, Pacific Studies Center
Lillian Kawasaki, Department of Environment, City of Los Angeles

Environmental Justice Resource Center, Clark-Atlanta University (July 20, 1995)
Atlanta, Georgia
Connie Tucker, Southern Organizing Committee for Economic & Social Justice
Sulaiman Madhi, African American Environmental Services Project
DeLane Garner, Environmental Justice Resource Center (Clark Atlanta University)

EPA staff who provided support during the public dialogues included:

EPA Region I: James Younger and John Podgurski
EPA Region III: John Armstead and Josie Matsinger
EPA Region IV: Barbara Dick and Vivian Malone-Jones
EPA Region V: Mardi Klev and Jim Bower
EPA Region IX: Sherry Nikzat and Dianna Young
EPA Headquarters: Jan Young, former Designated Federal Official for the NEJAC Waste and
                     Facility Siting Subcommittee, and Katherine Dawes, EPA National
                     Brownfields Team

Additional support in producing this report was provided by Victoria Robinson, PRC Environmental Management, Inc.

Addresses for the members of the community are provided below:

Sha King Alston
Program Manager
Center for Family Work & Community
1 University Avenue
Lowell, MA 01854
Phone: 508-934-4677
Fax: 508-934-3026

Grace Boggs
Detroit Summer
3061 Field St.
Detroit, MI 48214
Phone: 313-921-1236
Fax: 313-769-1449

DeLane Garner
Environmental Justice Resource Center
Clark Atlanta Universitry
223 James P. Brawley Drive, SW
Atlanta, GA 30314
Phone: 404-880-6920
Fax: 404-880-6909

Lillian Kawasaki
Los Angeles Department of the Environment
City Hall-Mail Stop 177
200 North Spring Street
Los Angeles, CA 90012
Phone: 213-580-1046
Fax: 213-580-1084

Sulaiman Madhi
African American Environmental Services
Project
233 Mitchell Street, Suite 410
Atlanta, GA 30303
Phone: 404-524-0357
Fax: 404-524-5851

Martha Matsuoka
The Urban Habitat Program
P.O. Box 29908
Presidio Station
Presidio Station of San Francisco
San Francisco, CA 94129-9908
Phone: 415-561-3335
Fax: 415-561-3334

Romel Pascal
The Urban Habitat Program
P.O. Box 29908
Presidio Station
San Francisco, CA 94129-9908
Phone: 415-561-3336
Fax: 415-561-3334

Maurice Sampson
Philadelphia Self-Reliant
129 West Gorgas Lane
Philadelphia, PA 19119
Phone: 215-686-9242
Fax: 215-686-9034

Lenny Siegel
Pacific Studies Center
222-B View Street
Mountain View, CA 94041
Phone: 415-968-8918
Fax: 415-968-1126

Sam Spofforth
Clean Water Action
1128 Walnut Street
Philadelphia, PA 19107
Phone: 215-629-4022
Fax: 215-629-3973

Connie Tucker
Southern Organizing committee for
Economic & Social Justice
P.O. Box 10518
Atlanta, GA 30310
Phone: 404-755-2855
Fax: 404-755-0575

Donele Wilkins
WARM Training Program
4835 Michigan Avenue
Detroit, MI 48210
Phone: 313-894-1030
Fax: 313-894-1063

Guy Williams
Environmental Defense Fund
1616 P Street, NW
Suite 150
Washington, D.C. 20036

**MEMBERS OF THE
NATIONAL ENVIRONMENTAL JUSTICE ADVISORY COUNCIL**

1995-96 List (25 Members)

Designated Federal Official (DFO)
Dr. Clarice Gaylord
Director
Office of Environmental Justice (3103)
U.S. Environmental Protection Agency
401 M Street, SW
Washington, DC 20460
(202) 260-6357

Dr. Robert Bullard
Environmental Justice Resource Center
Clark Atlanta University
223 Brawley Drive, SW
Atlanta, GA 30314

Dr. Mary R. English
Associate Director
Waste Management Research and Education
  Institute
327 South Stadium Hall
University of Tennessee
Knoxville, TN 37996

Dr. Richard Lazarus
Visiting Professor
Georgetown Unversity Law Center
600 New Jersey Avenue, NW
Washington, DC 20001

Dr. Beverly Wright
Deep South Center for Environmental Justice
Xavier University
8131 Aberdeen Road
New Orleans, LA 70126

Mr. John C. Borum
Vice President, Environment and Safety
Engineering
AT&T
131 Morristown Road
Basking Ridge, NJ 07920

Mr. Charles McDermott
Director of Governmental Affairs
Waste Management, Inc.
1155 Connecticut Avenue, NW, Suite 800
Washington, DC 20036

Chair
Mr. Richard Moore
Southwest Network for Environmental and
  Economic Justice
211 10th Street, SW
Albuquerque, NM 87102
(505) 242-0416

Mr. Lawrence G. Hurst
Director, Communications
Motorola, Inc.
Mail Drop R 3125
8220 East Roosevelt
Scottsdale, AZ 85257

Mr. Michael Pierle
Monsanto
800 North Lindburgh Street
St. Louis, MO 63167

Ms. Dolores Herrera
Executive Director
Albuquerque/San Jose Community Awareness
  Council, Inc.
2401 Broadway Boulevard, SE
Albuquerque, NM 87102-5009

Ms. Hazel Johnson
Executive Director
People for Community Recovery
13116 South Ellis Avenue
Chicago, IL 60627

Dr. Jean Sindab
National Council of Churches
475 Riverside Drive, Room 572
New York, NY 10115-0050

Mr. Charles Lee
Director of Research
United Church of Christ Commission for
  Racial Justice
475 Riverside Drive, 16th Floor
New York, NY 10015

Mr. John O'Leary, Esq.
Pierce Atwood
1 Monument Square
Portland, ME 04101

Mr. Baldemar Velasquez
Director
Farm Labor Organizing Committee
507 South St. Clair Street
Toledo, OH 43602

Mr. Haywood Turrentine
Laborers-AGC Education and Training Fund
P.O. Box 37
37 Deerfield Road
Pomfret Center, CT 06259

Honorable Salom•n Rond•n-Toll•ns
President, Natural Resources and
  Environmental Quality Commission
Capitolio San Juan, PR 00901

Ms. Velma Veloria
House of Representatives
Washington State Legislature
403 John L. O'Brien Building
P.O. Box 40622
Olympia, WA 98504-0622
   OR   1511 South Ferdinand Street
           Seattle, WA 98108

Mr. Arthur Ray, Esq.
Deputy Director
Maryland Department of the Environment
2500 Broening Highway
Baltimore, MD 21224

Ms. Gail Small
Executive Director
Native Action
Box 316
Lame Deer, MT 59043

Ms. Jean Gamache, Esq.
Tlignit and Haida Indian Tribes of Alaska
125 Christensen Drive
P.O. Box 104432
Anchorage, AK 99510

Mr. Walter Bresette
Lake Superior Chippewa
Route 1, Box 117
Bayfield, WI 54814

Ms. Peggy Saika
Asian Pacific Environment Network
3126 California Street
Oakland, CA 94602

Ms. Nathalie Walker
Sierra Club Legal Defense Fund
400 Magazine Street, Suite 401
New Orleans, LA 70130

Ms. Deeohn Ferris
Washington Office for Environmental
  Justice
1511 K Street, NW, Suite 1026
Washington, DC 20005

MEMBERS OF THE
WASTE AND FACILITY SITING SUBCOMMITTEE
NATIONAL ENVIRONMENTAL JUSTICE ADVISORY COUNCIL

1995-96 List (15 Members)

Designated Federal Official (DFO)
Mr. Kent Benjamin
Office of Solid Waste and Emergency
Response
U.S. Environmental Protection Agency
401 M Street, SW (MC 5101)
Washington, DC 20460
(202) 260-1692
e-mail: benjamin.kent@epamail.epa.gov

Ms. Sue Briggum
WMX Technologies, Inc.
1155 Connecticut Avenue, NW, Suite 800
Washington, DC 20036

Ms. Teresa Cordova, PhD
University of New Mexico
Community and Regional Planning Program
School of Architecture and Planning
2414 Central Avenue, SE
Albuquerque, NM 87131

Mr. Donald Elisburg
Donald Elisburg Law Offices
11713 Rosalinda Drive
Potomac, MD 20854-3531

Mr. Tom Goldtooth
Red Band of Chippewa Indians
P.O. Box 485
Albuquerque, NM 87102

Mr. Michael Guerrero
SW Organizing Project
211 10th Street, SW
Bemjidi, MN 56601

Mr. David Hahn-Baker
Inside Out, Inc.
440 Lincoln Parkway
Buffalo, NY 14216

Ms. Lillian Kawasaki
Los Angeles Department of the Environment
City Hall-Mail Stop 177
200 North Spring Street
Los Angeles, CA 90012

Chair
Charles Lee
Director of Research
United Church of Christ Commission for Racial
Justice
475 Riverside Drive, 16th Floor
New York, NY 10015
(212) 870-2077
e-mail: 103001.2273@compuserve.com

Mr. Tom Kennedy
Association of State and Territorial Solid
 Waste Management Officials
444 North Capitol Street, Suite 388
Washington, DC 20001

Mr. Scott Kayla Morrison
President
Choctaws for Democracy
P. O. Box 11
Talinia, OK 74571

Mr. Jon Sesso
Planning Director
Silverbow Mt. Planning Committee
155 West Granite Street
Butte, MT 59701

Mr. Lenny Siegel
Pacific Studies Center
222-B View Street
Mountain View, CA 94041

Dr. Jean Sindab
Director
National Council of Churches
475 Riverside Drive, Room 572
New York, NY 10115-0050

Ms. Connie Tucker
Southern Organizing Committee
P.O. Box 10518
Atlanta, GA 30310

Ms. Nathalie Walker
Sierra Club Legal Defense Fund
400 Magazine Street, Suite 401
New Orleans, LA 70130

LIST OF EPA BROWNFIELDS PILOT SITES
Through November 1996
*•Economic development and environmental
protection must go hand-in-hand•*

National Pilots

Baltimore, MD
Birmingham, AL
Bridgeport, CT
Burlington, VT
Cape Charles-Northampton County, VA
Charlotte, NC
Chicopee, MA
Chippewa County/Kinross Township, MI
Cleveland, OH
Detroit, MI
Emeryville, CA
Houston, TX
Indianapolis, IN
Kansas City, KS and MO
Knoxville, TN
Laredo, TX
Lawrence, MA
Lima, OH
Louisville, KY
Lowell, MA

Navajo Nation
Newark, NJ
New Orleans, LA
New York, NY
Oregon Mill Sites, OR
Phoenixville, PA
Portland, OR
Rhode Island
Richmond, CA
Richmond, VA
Rochester, NY
Rome, NY
Sacramento, CA
St. Louis, MO
Stockton, CA
Tacoma, WA
Trenton, NJ
West Central Municipal Conference, IL
Worcester, MA

Regional Pilots

Atlanta, GA
Bellingham, WA
Bonne Terre, MO
Boston, MA
Buffalo, NY
Camden, NJ
Cincinnati, OH
Clearwater, FL
Concord, NH
Dallas, TX
Downriver Community Conference, MI
Duwamish, WA
East St. Louis, IL
State of Illinois
State of Indiana
Kalamazoo, MI
Miami, FL
State of Minnesota
Murray City, UT

Naugatuck Valley, CT
New Haven, CT
Northwest Indiana Cities
Oakland, CA
Panhandle Health District, ID
Philadelphia, PA
Pittsburgh, PA
Portland, ME
Prichard, AL
Provo, UT
Puyallup Tribe of Tacoma, WA
Salt Lake City, UT
Sand Creek Corridor, CO
San Francisco, CA
Shreveport, LA
Sioux Falls, SD
Somerville, MA
West Jordan, UT

KEY EPA ACTIONS TO DATE

This is a list of the several key actions EPA has undertaken related to the Brownfields Initiative.

Informed and Empowered Community

Community Involvement in Brownfields pilot projects

6/95   Initiated the •community involvement check-up,• as an ongoing part of the Brownfields national pilot application process to confirm the participation of the local community organizations and representatives. (This was in response to recommendations made at the Philadelphia Public Dialogue.)

8/95   Developed a Response to the NEJAC •Resolution on Environmental Justice and Urban Revitalization• for review by the Federal Interagency Working Group (IWG) on Environmental Justice.

9/95   Integrated comments from NEJAC subcommittee members in the revised version of the •Application Guidelines• booklet for the Brownfields national pilots.

2/96   Sponsored the •Brownfields Pilots National Workshop• which used the NEJAC working draft Public Dialogue report to develop the breakout sessions• agendas. EPA sponsored the participation of community representatives from Oakland, CA; Detroit, MI; and Boston, MA.

Job Creation, Training, and Career Development

Training Programs (Teacher•s Institute, Rio Hondo, HMTRI, NIEHS, Superfund Step-Up, Cuyahoga Community College, Department of Labor)

TEACHER•S INSTITUTE

6/95   Conducted the third EPA-Morgan State University Summer Environmental Teachers Institute, in Baltimore, Maryland (40 teachers from across the country attended).

1/96   Awarded a cooperative agreement to Morgan State University to sponsor the fourth Summer Environmental Teachers Institute, scheduled for July 7-19 in Baltimore, Maryland.

RIO HONDO COLLEGE

8/95   Established the Rio Hondo College Environmental Education and Training Center in Whitter, California. The college began work on this project in March, 1995, through a cooperative agreement with EPA, to provide environmental job training and placement for local residents and has an 85% minority enrollment.

HMTRI Continued to sponsor job training and development and community outreach activities linked to the Brownfields Initiative, by working with the Hazardous Materials Training and Research Institute (HMTRI) to expand training and curriculum development to community colleges located near brownfields pilots.

11/95   Sponsored a HMTRI workshop in Baltimore, Maryland which was attended by 17 community colleges located near Brownfields pilot sites.

2/96   Invited HMTRI to participate in the Brownfields Pilots National Workshop Showcase in order to conduct outreach to EPA brownfields pilots and other stakeholders.

3/96   Awarded a cooperative agreement to HMTRI to continue providing workshops, curriculum and technical assistance to community colleges located near brownfields communities.

7/96   HMTRI workshop to be held in St. Louis, MO. Twenty brownfields community colleges   are scheduled to attend, along with representatives form the St. Louis Brownfields pilots, the St. Louis Private Industry Council, and organized labor.

NIEHS   EPA is working with the National Institute of Environmental Health Sciences (NIEHS) to ensure the minority worker training grants - established to facilitate the development of urban minority youth worker training programs - overlap with Brownfields pilot communities (e.g., Cleveland, New Orleans).

CUYAHOGA COMMUNITY COLLEGE

EPA continues to sponsor job training, education and outreach activities related to Brownfields at Cuyahoga Community College (TRI-C) in Cleveland, Ohio. In addition, TRI-C was awarded a NIEHS Minority Worker Training Program grant, through Laborers AGC, which should enhance job training activity in the Cleveland area.

SUPERFUND STEP-UP

The Superfund Step-Up Program is designed as a partnership between EPA, HUD, and DOL to collaborate in facilitating training and employment opportunities for community residents in the environmental cleanup field. The program is designed to encourage contractors, labor organizations, where applicable, and other sponsors to involve community residents in the benefits of environmental cleanup and related activities.

DEPARTMENT OF LABOR

EPA and DOL's Employment and Training Administration (ETA) are working together to link EPA local brownfields contacts with local Job Training Partnership Act (JTPA) funded organizations, such as Private Industry Councils. The partnership between the two agencies focuses on creating mechanisms to promote local hiring at brownfields sites.

Community/Private Sector Partnerships

EPA Intergovernmental Personnel Assignments

EPA has assigned eight staff members, though IPAs, to help develop State and local Brownfields programs. Currently, two staff members are assigned with the States of Illinois and Colorado, and one each to Dallas, TX; Detroit, MI; East Chicago, IN; East Palo Alto, CA; and Los Angeles, CA.

State, Local, Tribal, and Territorial Governments

Partnerships with Local Government Partners

International City/County Management Association (ICMA)

ICMA is an international professional and education organization for appointed administrators and assistant administrators who serve cities, counties, district, and regions. ICMA recently entered into a cooperative agreement with EPA to develop a CD ROM resource for municipalities involved in Brownfields cleanup and redevelopment activities.

Northeast-Midwest Institute

> The Northeast-Midwest Institute is a non-profit research and public education organization dedicated to the long-term economic vitality of the Northeastern and Midwestern States. They do research, develop public policies to address the economic barriers to Brownfields, write case studies, sponsor regional conferences and distribute publications. They wrote the first comprehensive analysis of the Brownfields issue in 1991 and are working with EPA on a cooperative agreement to develop case studies on current Brownfields pilots and previous Brownfields activities captured in one of their earlier reports. Results will be communicated through constituent education briefings held in the east, Midwest and western regions of the US, sponsored by Members of Congress.

Federal Interagency Cooperation, etc.

Joint Research with the Department of Housing and Urban Development

> EPA and HUD are funding a joint cooperative agreement to research the effect contamination has on property values

Memorandum of Understanding's with Federal Partners

Housing and Urban Development (HUD)

> Singed a MOU with the Department of Housing and Urban Development (HUD) to partner on the Superfund Step-Up apprenticeship training program for economically disadvantaged persons living in the vicinity of Superfund Sites.

Economic Development Administration (EDA)

> EPA signed a MOU with EDA of the Department of Commerce to consult on economic redevelopment and reuse of Brownfields to ensure that sound environmental and economic development principles are followed, and to share knowledge and serve on advisory groups regarding Brownfields projects.

U.S. Department of Labor (DOL)

> Anticipate signing of a memorandum of understanding in the Summer of 1996 with the Department of Labor's Employment and Training Administration (ETA) which will foster coordination on workforce development activities related to the Brownfields program.

> Expect to finalize MOU with the Department of Labor's Bureau of Apprenticeship and Training (BAT) on the Superfund Step-Up Apprenticeship Training Program during the Summer of 1996.

U.S. Department of the Interior

> EPA is working on development of a Memorandum of Understanding (MOU) with the Rivers and Trails Assistance Office of the Department of Interior (under the U.S. Park Service). The MOU will encourage effective collaboration at Brownfields Pilots and long term sustainability at these sites by testing community driven non-profit approaches such as those used by the GroundWork Trust of England, numerous Redevelopment Authorities and other Community Development Corporations. DOI's contributions include urban beautification activities, enhancement of amenities such as green spaces, public places, parks and trails, and remediation/revitalization/redevelopment activities underway through the Brownfields pilots and other locations.